ENDANGERED PLANET

Previous page: A logger saws through a rainforest
tree trunk, Cameroon, central Africa.

▼ Built in a disused quarry in Cornwall, southern England,
the Eden Project is home to over 5,000 kinds of plant from
all the different climatic zones of the world. Plants are vital
for life on earth, because they collect the sun's energy and
release the oxygen that we breathe. The Eden Project spells
out an important message: we need plants, but at the same
time we are making it hard for many of them to survive.

KFK · KINGFISHER KNOWLEDGE

ENDANGERED PLANET

David Burnie

Foreword by
Tony Juniper

KINGFISHER

Managing editor: Russell Mclean
Senior designer: Peter Clayman
Picture researcher: Kate Miller
Production controller: Lindsey Scott
DTP manager: Nicky Studdart
Artwork archivists: Wendy Allison, Jenny Lord
Proofreader: Jennifer Schofield
Indexer: Sue Lightfoot

KINGFISHER
Kingfisher Publications Plc, New Penderel House,
283–288 High Holborn, London WC1V 7HZ
www.kingfisherpub.com

First published by Kingfisher Publications Plc 2004

10 9 8 7 6 5 4 3 2 1

1TR/0604/TWP/MA(MA)/130ENSOMA/F

ISBN 0 7534 0962 3

Contents

GO FURTHER...
INFORMATION PANEL KEY:

 websites and
further reading

career paths

places to visit

NOTE TO READERS
The website addresses listed in this book are correct at the time of going to print. However, due
to the ever-changing nature of the internet, website addresses and content can change. Websites
can contain links that are unsuitable for children. The publisher cannot be held responsible for
changes in website addresses or content, or for information obtained through third-party websites.
We strongly advise that internet searches should be supervised by an adult.

▼ Pools of oil surround drilling rigs in Azerbaijan, on the edge of the Caspian Sea.
This central Asian country contains some of the most polluted shores in the world.

Foreword

Never before in the long history of the earth has one species – humankind – had such a dramatic impact on the planet that sustains all known life. Recent decades in particular have seen a rapid acceleration in the rate of environmental change. Today, people are altering the world's climate and using up more resources than ever before. We are even on the verge of causing the extinction of more species than at any time since the dinosaurs disappeared, about 66 million years ago.

Each year, the world's growing population demands more food, energy, household products, fresh water, places to live, cars and roads. All of these things cause some impact on the world around us. Forests and wetlands are cleared to make way for farms, mines are dug out to reach minerals, harmful pollution is released from different industries, while the use of energy in our houses, cars and factories is causing changes to the climate.

My environmental work has taken me to many different countries, and in each place the challenges are different. In very poor countries, people need to find ways to provide food, water and housing while still preserving their amazing rainforests and other wildlife habitats. In rich countries, the environment could be better protected by cutting pollution, saving energy and using fewer resources – by recycling more, for example. In the end though, every single one of us relies on the same earth, and so all of us need to help look after it, no matter where we live.

When I was a child, and first became aware of threats to the environment, few people knew about pollution or disappearing wildlife. Today, things are different. More and more people know that they must work harder to look after the world, and they are making changes to do just that. Where I live, in England, some kinds of pollution have been cleaned up or reduced and some wild animals are coming back after nearly disappearing for good.

Saving the environment is really about common sense: making sure the best places for wildlife are looked after, reducing waste, using cars less often, saving energy and using the best new technologies to minimize pollution. But most important of all, it is about looking after people – especially the world's poorest people. Giving everyone in the world a good life, while keeping all of the wildlife, stopping pollution and not changing the climate, is a huge challenge. But it can be done.

During the many years that I have worked to save the environment, I have seen a lot of different solutions and met many people who know how to solve environmental problems. But saving the environment is not just for experts. Everyone needs to play a part, because all of the big environmental issues are caused and solved by the little things done by you and me. So read this fascinating book and learn something about the big questions facing every one of us who lives on this small planet. Above all, don't be worried, but do think about how you can do your bit to help. It's a beautiful world – let's look after it.

Tony Juniper, Executive Director, Friends of the Earth
www.foe.co.uk, www.foei.org

Ring-tailed lemur, Madagascar

CHAPTER 1

Fragile earth

By the time you read this book, life may have been found on another planet – the most likely place being Mars. The chances look slim, but if this happens, it will be an incredibly important event, because it will mean that the earth is not alone. From all we know about the universe, earth-like planets are rare. If space exploration does uncover alien life, it is likely to be simple and microscopic, like the bacteria on earth today. Our planet has harboured life for nearly four billion years, and during that time millions of different species have developed. Life has adapted to all kinds of changes, from ice ages to catastrophic meteorite strikes. But after this long and varied past, something remarkable has happened: a species has evolved that dominates earth. That species is us, and the earth's future is in our hands.

The living planet

Life on earth almost certainly began by accident, through a chain of chemical reactions that took place over an immense period of time. But why did life take hold here, and not on any other planet that we have studied? One reason is that the earth is just the right distance from the sun. It gets enough heat to keep it warm, but not so much that it fries. Earth also has an atmosphere, which protects the surface from harmful rays. Finally, it is covered by water – a perfect substance for cradling living things.

▲ Earth's atmosphere is like a protective cloak that shields living things. The northern lights – seen here over Alaska – are caused by high-energy particles from the sun that plunge into our atmosphere.

▶ This diagram shows the thinness of the biosphere compared to the planet as a whole. The biosphere is like a living skin, stretched over the entire surface of the earth.

The biosphere
Although the earth is home to life, more than 99.999 per cent of the planet is strictly off-limits to living things. The outer atmosphere is much too cold, while most of the earth's crust is far too hot. Sandwiched in between is the biosphere – a zone where living things can survive. Compared to the entire planet, the biosphere is extremely thin. At its deepest, it measures just 25km from top to bottom, or about 45 times the height of the tallest structure ever built. This wraparound layer is our home, and it is one that we share with every other form of life on earth. Inside the biosphere, matter and energy are constantly on the move. Vital substances, such as water and carbon, shuttle between living things and their surroundings, while energy pours into the biosphere from the sun. All around planet earth, the whole biosphere bustles with growth and activity.

Energy and living things

Energy is the driving force that keeps living things working. Our energy comes from food, but the things that we eat also have to collect energy. If you trace your way back through this chain of energy, you end up with plants. Instead of getting energy from other living things, plants make it for themselves by a process called photosynthesis, which takes place in their leaves. Through photosynthesis, plants trap the energy in sunlight, and use it to build substances that they need to grow. This remarkable trick is also performed by microscopic algae, which drift in untold billions throughout the seas. Because photosynthesis creates food, it powers almost all life on earth. If it stopped tomorrow, every living thing – apart from a few specialized bacteria – would slowly but surely die out.

Is there life elsewhere?

Despite years of listening, looking and waiting, scientists have detected no signs of life beyond our own solar system. Many experts think that it exists, but with such vast distances separating us from other stars, their hunch cannot be proved. Within the solar system, the task is much easier, because probes can visit other planets and search them for signs of life. So far, this exploration has revealed some tantalizing hints of past life on Mars, but no definite proof. Farther away, some of the moons of Jupiter and Saturn seem to contain liquid water, which would make it just possible that life could have started here. The hunt continues but, so far, we have no positive results – our planet seems to be unique.

▲ In 1996, NASA scientists announced that the yellow objects on this Martian meteorite could be the fossils of ancient bacteria. Since then, most experts have changed their minds. In spite of this rethink, Mars still looks to be the most promising place for life beyond earth.

◀ As the sun sets over Africa's grasslands, plants and animals put its energy to work. Plants collect only about one per cent of the solar energy that falls on earth, but this is enough to power almost every living thing on the planet. The only exceptions are certain bacteria, which get energy from minerals in the earth's crust.

Natural cycles

When a river plunges over a waterfall, it is playing a part in an endless cycle that keeps all the world's water on the move. Although we cannot see it, many other essential substances, such as carbon and nitrogen, move in cycles too. These natural cycles are vital for living things, because they deliver life's chemical ingredients, and take them away after they have been used.

▲ At the Niagara Falls, between Canada and the USA, water plunges nearly 60m on its journey towards the sea. Freshwater makes up less than one per cent of all the liquid water in the world.

The water cycle

Every day, the sun's energy evaporates about 1,000 billion tonnes of water from the world's seas. This incredible lifting operation marks the start of the hydrological cycle, or water cycle. From here on, things literally go downhill. The water vapour condenses into clouds that produce rain or snow. Sooner or later, this moisture makes its way back to the sea. The water cycle is crucial to all life, but it is particularly important on land. Here, rainfall helps to shape the world's living communities, or biomes (see page 15). The water cycle also shapes the surface of the earth, because rain slowly erodes even the hardest rocks, creating valleys and flood plains as it sweeps sediment towards the sea.

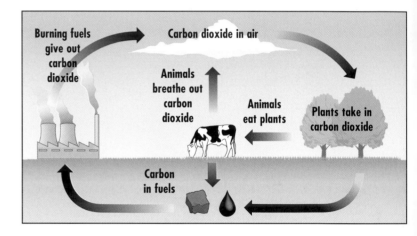

▲ This simplified version of the carbon cycle shows how carbon dioxide shuttles between the air and living things. In other parts of the cycle, carbon dioxide is absorbed and released by the sea. Some of this carbon becomes built in to seabed sediment, which is then transformed into rocks.

The carbon cycle

Life is based on carbon, a chemical element that is amazingly good at forming different compounds (mixtures of two or more chemical ingredients). On earth, pure carbon is rare. Instead, the carbon cycle centres around carbon dioxide, a gas that makes up about 0.03 per cent of the atmosphere. With the help of energy from sunlight, plants collect this gas, and they build it into complex carbon compounds that they use to grow. When animals eat plants – or each other – the reverse happens: carbon compounds are broken down, and their energy and carbon dioxide are released. This part of the cycle is fast, but carbon sometimes becomes locked up for millions of years. This happens when dead remains become buried, and slowly turn into coal or oil. If these fuels are dug up and burned, ancient carbon suddenly floods back into the air.

▲ During a forest fire, the carbon stored in living trees is suddenly combined with oxygen and released back into the air as carbon dioxide. Plants also release their carbon when they die, as microbes – tiny living things, such as bacteria – gradually break them down.

◀ Like beads on a necklace, nodules sprout from the roots of a pea plant. Each nodule contains millions of nitrogen-fixing bacteria which help the plant to grow. The plant forms the nodules to encourage bacteria to move in.

The nitrogen cycle

Unlike carbon dioxide, nitrogen is extremely plentiful, making up 78 per cent of the atmosphere. All living things need it but, strangely, very few can use pure nitrogen from the air. Instead, plants collect nitrogen that has been 'fixed', or chemically converted, by bacteria living in the soil. Animals get their nitrogen by eating plants or each other. When living things die, the return half of the cycle begins. The dead remains are broken down and, thanks to yet more bacteria, nitrogen finds its way back into the air. For humans, the nitrogen cycle is very important, because it affects how well plants grow. Some plants have their own nitrogen supply, thanks to nitrogen-fixing bacteria that live in their roots. These plants – such as clover, peas and beans – have been grown for generations as a way of improving the fertility of the soil. Today, nitrogen is also fixed industrially, to make synthetic fertilizer.

▲ Lightning 'fixes' nitrogen when it flashes through the sky. Later, when it rains, this fixed nitrogen is washed into the soil. Nitrogen is also fixed by cars, which pump it out of their exhausts.

Evolution

How many kinds of living things are there on earth? Three centuries ago, when scientists first began to ask this question, they thought that the total was less than 10,000. Today, we know this is a vast underestimate. Nearly two million different species have already been identified, and it is possible that ten times that number are still waiting to be discovered. This amazing richness has come about through evolution – a process that allows living things to adapt gradually to different ways of life.

▼ By looking at fossils and comparing their features, palaeontologists can often work out the path that evolution has followed. This 'family tree' shows the saurischian (lizard-hipped) dinosaurs, which evolved from a single shared ancestor over 200 million years ago. One group of these dinosaurs gave rise to modern birds.

Tertiary period
66–1.6 mya
(million years ago)

Birds

Cretaceous period
144–66 mya

Sauropods

Dromaeosaurs

Tyrannosaurs

Allosaurs

Ceratosaurs

Jurassic period
208–144 mya

Triassic period
245–208 mya

Evolution and adaptation

All living things can copy themselves, or reproduce. But, unlike factories, they hardly ever turn out the same product more than once. Instead, their offspring vary, because each one inherits a slightly different set of genes. A factory that worked like this would not last for long, but in the world of nature the opposite is true. In the struggle to survive, variety is often an advantage, because it means that some individuals have a better chance of surviving and leaving lots of young. If their offspring are also successful at breeding, their winning features become more and more widespread, while less successful ones die out. As a result, the whole species gradually changes over many generations, building up adaptations that help it to thrive. In other words, it evolves.

◄ As they evolve, species sometimes become close partners. For example, hummingbirds have evolved a partnership with bromeliad plants. In return for nectar, hummingbirds carry pollen from plant to plant.

The life and death of species

If you think of life as a bush, species are the very tips of its twigs. Since life first appeared, the bush has kept expanding, because many new species have evolved. The bush also has lots of dead-end branches, however, where species have become extinct. Extinction is a natural process that usually happens gradually, but just occasionally natural catastrophes have swept away thousands of species at one time. The last of these mass extinctions occurred 66 million years ago, at the end of the dinosaur age (see page 17).

Measuring biodiversity

Evolution works so slowly that losing species is a serious business. Today, the extinction rate is on the rise, so biologists are urgently counting the species that we have. So far, about 4,500 kinds of mammals and 9,500 birds have been identified. These groups of animals have been well studied, so it is unlikely that many more will be found. But with some groups, such as insects and deep-sea fish, the work has only just begun. If the extinction rate keeps climbing, many species could die out before they are found.

Biodiversity hotspots

In some places, called biodiversity hotspots, evolution seems to have gone into overdrive. They contain a richness of life out of all proportion to their size. For example, South Africa's Cape Province is home to an astounding 8,000 species of plants, two-thirds of which live nowhere else. Brazil's Atlantic forest is a hotspot for plants and monkeys, while Madagascar has five families of primates that are unique to that part of the world.

► This map shows the world's biodiversity hotspots – regions that have an unusually rich variety of species, including many that live nowhere else. Many hotspots have been damaged by human activities, which makes it all the more important to protect the areas that remain.

California, USA
Canaries
Mediterranean
Caucasus
Southwestern China
Hawaii
Caribbean
Indo-Burma
Mesoamerica
Guinean forests
Western Ghats and Sri Lanka
Philippines
Galapagos
Polynesia and Micronesia
Western Ecuador
Brazilian cerrado
Sunda region
Andes mountains
Madagascar
Atlantic forest, Brazil
Cape Province, South Africa
Southwestern Australia
Central Chile
New Zealand

▲ Suspended from a hot-air balloon, an inflatable sledge allows biologists to examine the rainforest canopy as they search for undiscovered species. The scientists are working in Gabon – a central African country that still contains large expanses of unspoilt forest.

Homes and habitats

Even without modern technology, humans can survive in mountains, in deserts, and on land close to the poles. With it, we can endure some really hostile environments, such as the deep sea or space. But we are very much an exception. Unlike us, most of the world's living things have adapted for survival in one habitat alone. This kind of specialization helps to shape the global map of life.

Habitats

Habitats include a wealth of different surroundings, from open grassland to seafloor mud. Unlike a home, a habitat normally supplies all the resources that a living thing needs. This does not mean just the obvious things, such as space, food and daylight, but also some obscure ones, such as the level of rare minerals in the soil. An ideal habitat for one species can be less than ideal for others. For example, some bacteria flourish in hot springs containing dilute sulphuric acid. In this extreme habitat, any fish would quickly dissolve.

KEY TO MAP
- Polar
- Arctic tundra
- Mountains
- Coniferous forests
- Temperate forests
- Grasslands and savanna
- Shrublands
- Deserts
- Wetlands
- Tropical forests
- Coral reefs

◄ ▲ Brown pelicans live in a coastal habitat (shown in orange). On South America's east coast, they do not live farther south than the mouth of the River Amazon, because here the mud-laden water prevents them from spotting food.

A place on the map

Because hot springs always occur in volcanic regions, this is the only place where acid-proof bacteria are found. In the same way, the distribution of other species is fixed by the conditions that they need. For example, brown pelicans feed by dive-bombing fish, so they must have clear water to see their prey. Avocets, on the other hand, have beaks with sensitive tips, so these birds can feed in water that is as cloudy as a cup of tea. Sometimes the distribution of one species controls the distribution of another. Robber crabs feed mainly on coconuts, so they are found only in parts of the tropics where coconuts grow. On an even bigger scale, coral reefs are found only in warm-water regions, so all the animals that depend on coral need warm water too.

ARCTIC OCEAN

Norwegian Sea

Barents Sea

Kara Sea

Laptev Sea

East Siberian Sea

Arctic Circle

EUROPE

ASIA

PACIFIC OCEAN

Mediterranean Sea

Tropic of Cancer

AFRICA

Arabian Sea

Bay of Bengal

Philippine Sea

Gulf of Guinea

Equator

INDIAN OCEAN

Tropic of Capricorn

AUSTRALASIA AND OCEANIA

SOUTHERN OCEAN

Antarctic Circle

ANTARCTICA

Biomes

Despite its local differences, life shows many similarities right across the globe. African rainforest looks very similar to Asian rainforest, even though it contains quite different animals and plants. In the same way, American grassland has a lot in common with Australian grassland, even though they are on opposite sides of the planet. These worldwide mixtures of plants and animals are known as biomes; unlike habitats, they are big and clear enough to be visible from space. After biomes, there is only one more step up in scale, to the biosphere – the complete collection of all the places where living things are found.

◀ This map shows all the major biomes of the world, as they were before humans started to clear land for farming. Biomes are shaped mainly by climate, because this affects the kind of plants that can grow in any particular place.

▶ Giant tortoises have evolved several times, often on remote tropical islands. This specimen is from the Galapagos, where the heaviest adults can weigh over 250kg. Its long neck enables it to stretch high into plants to reach food.

Local specialities

Many habitat types are scattered right across the globe, so you might expect their inhabitants to be worldwide as well. A few species – such as the barn owl – are truly global, but most are tied to a particular part of the planet. Giant tortoises live on volcanic slopes in the Galapagos Islands, but not on the same kind of slopes in South America, 800km away. The reason for this is that every species originally evolves in one place. Some manage to spread far from their birthplace, but many are shut in by barriers, such as mountains or sea. These obstacles divide the world up into separate regions, each with species that are found there and nowhere else. Remote islands – such as the Galapagos and New Zealand – are particularly rich in these 'endemic' species. Unfortunately, endemic species often suffer when plants and animals are introduced from outside.

▶ Spinifex grassland covers much of the Australian outback. This drought-resistant plant grows in scattered clumps, which provide shelter and food for animals. One bird – the spinifex pigeon – is nearly always found where this grass grows.

Coping with change

It is hard to imagine anything more delicate than a butterfly, as it flutters from flower to flower, or something more helpless than an antelope with a pride of lions on its trail. But simply by existing, creatures like this prove that they are a lot tougher than they seem. Like all living things, their ancestors adapted to a changing world, and they do the same when they breed and pass on their genes. But today's species also have to cope with something new: worldwide changes brought about by human beings.

▲ In Arizona's Petrified Forest, USA, fossilized tree trunks are scattered over the desert floor. These remains show that the climate here was once much more moist than it is today.

An unpredictable world

The earth is always changing in different ways. Some changes follow predictable rhythms, meaning that living things can keep in step. These rhythms include the shifting seasons, the tides, and the 24-hour cycle of night and day. But far bigger changes are also afoot. Continents creep across the planet's surface, ice ages come and go, and sea levels rise and fall. Unlike seasons, these do not follow a clear-cut pattern, so no one can forecast exactly where they are heading. For living things, these changes can be a problem, but they open up new opportunities too.

Continental drift

The earth's outer crust is cool, but a huge amount of heat is locked up in its core. This heat is the cause of volcanoes and earthquakes, and it keeps all the continents on the move. Continental drift is an incredibly slow process: the fastest mover – South America – travels at less than 20cm a year. But, over millions of years, this movement transforms the planet's surface, splitting and joining continents and the wildlife they have aboard. Continental drift is an important force in evolution, because it separates groups of plants or animals, giving them a chance to develop in different ways.

Climate change

Scientists know how continents move, but long-term climate change is harder to explain. Ice ages may be triggered by changes in the earth's orbit, or by clouds of dust that volcanoes eject into the air. Continental drift could also play a part, by blocking warm sea currents that carry heat towards the poles. Whatever the cause, these swings in climate can be dramatic. At the height of the last ice age, 18,000 years ago, ice sheets spread as far as southern England. Today, on the other hand, most of the world's glaciers are shrinking fast.

◀ Between1980 (far left) and 2002 (left), Peru's Jacabamba glacier melted and receded as the world's climate warmed. The climate has often warmed in the past, through natural changes, but this time human activities seem to be the cause.

▲ Two hundred million years ago, the world's continents were joined together in a giant landmass called Pangaea (above right), which later broke apart as the continents drifted towards their present positions (above left). Pangaea itself was formed when ancient continents collided, much further back in time.

▶ Volcanic eruptions can trigger mass extinctions, by throwing huge amounts of dust into the air. The dust can block sunlight for many years, making it difficult for plants to grow.

Life on the move

Climate change works much faster than continental drift, but even so, living things manage to adapt to it and survive. Animals adapt to cold by evolving better insulation, or by hibernating for many months each year. Plants often adapt by moving – something they can do by spreading their seeds. In cold conditions, Arctic tundra expands, while northern forests migrate southwards and tropical forests shrink. In warmer and wetter times, the reverse happens. Changes like these mean that the world's vegetation never stays the same for long. Instead, entire biomes react to the changing climate, just as if they were single living things.

Mass extinctions

Occasionally in life's history, disaster strikes, and a catastrophic event rocks the world. For example, 66 million years ago, a giant meteorite smashed into the earth, wiping out a large slice of life, including the dinosaurs. Faced with this kind of calamity, species do not have time to adjust – the best they can hope for is to survive. Fortunately, mass extinctions are extremely rare events, but their effects can be severe. Nearly 250 million years ago, the largest mass extinction of all wiped out over two-thirds of the species on earth. Life eventually recovered, but the process took millions of years.

SUMMARY OF CHAPTER 1: FRAGILE EARTH

Conditions for life

This chapter looked at one of the most important questions in science: why does life exist on our planet, but nowhere else that we know of? The answer is that earth had the right mix of conditions for life to appear: it is the right distance from the sun, it has a protective atmosphere, and much of the planet's surface is covered by water. Once life began, it managed to adapt and evolve, and it has been doing this successfully for nearly four billion years. Life may exist elsewhere – Mars seems to be the most likely place – but it has not yet been found.

The biosphere

Although the earth is huge, only a small fraction of the planet – known as the biosphere – is actually home to living things.

Giant tortoise, Galapagos Islands

In the biosphere, the sun's energy provides the driving force that keeps living things alive. It also provides the energy that keeps carbon and other vital substances on the move. The only things that use sunlight directly are plants – through a process called photosynthesis – and some specialized bacteria. Animals get their energy indirectly, by eating plants or other living things.

Patterns of life

Over long periods of time, living things slowly change, or evolve. Evolution does not happen in a single lifetime. Instead, it occurs over many generations, as each species adapts to its surroundings. During evolution, new species sometimes develop, and existing ones eventually become extinct. Evolution allows living things to cope with long-term changes, such as ice ages and continental drift. It also creates biomes – the characteristic mixtures of plants and animals that exist all over the world. On rare occasions, however, large slices of earth's life have been wiped out by cataclysmic natural events, such as meteorite strikes and massive volcanic eruptions.

Go further...

Take a trip through earth's history by visiting this online time machine: www.ucmp.berkeley.edu/help/timeform.html

Discover up-to-date information about the search for extraterrestrial life at: www.seti-inst.edu

Find out more about the world's biodiversity hotspots by exploring this interactive map: www.biodiversityhotspots.org/xp/Hotspots/home/interactive_map.xml

The Kingfisher Book of Evolution by Stephen Webster (Kingfisher, 2000)

Atlas of the Prehistoric World by Douglas Palmer (Marshall Publishing, 2000)

Biologist
Studies living things and the way that they work.

Ecologist
Examines the connections between different kinds of living things, and the environment in which they live.

Exobiologist
Studies the origin of life, and its possible existence on other planets.

Glaciologist
Examines ice and frozen landscapes, and the effects of ice ages in the past.

Palaeontologist
Investigates prehistoric life by examining fossils that living things have left behind.

Visit London's Natural History Museum, where permanent exhibitions explain how life has evolved and how the process of evolution was discovered:
The Natural History Museum
Cromwell Road,
London SW7 5BD, UK
Telephone: +44 (0) 20 7942 5011
www.nhm.ac.uk

Find out about ecology and conservation by visiting the Eden Project, one of Britain's most fascinating days out:
The Eden Project
Bodelva, St Austell
Cornwall PL24 2SG, UK
Telephone: +44 (0) 1726 811911
www.edenproject.com

CHAPTER 2

Flooded village, Tana river valley, Kenya

Planet under pressure

Five centuries ago, European explorers
made the first ever round-the-world
voyage. It took three years. Today, jet
planes circle the earth in a thousandth of
that time. Satellites can take less than an
hour. These comparisons show something
we are all becoming aware of: the earth
is a relatively small planet, and our impact
on it is growing. Thanks to our booming
population, and to advances in science

we are affecting the way the entire world
works. Part of our impact comes from the
resources we use, such as energy, water and
space. The more we take, the less there is
for other living things. Just as important
is the waste we produce, from household
rubbish to car exhaust fumes. Some of
this stays close to home, but some travels
through the oceans and the atmosphere,
where it can have far-reaching effects.

An escalating impact

Half a million years ago, when our species first appeared, the human population was small and people had very little impact on the planet. But since then, three great breakthroughs have dramatically increased our effects on the world around us. The first was the agricultural revolution, which took place about 10,000 years ago, when people first learned how to farm. The second was the industrial revolution, which began in the early 1700s, while the third – the information revolution – is happening now.

▶ Lined up in the desert of New Mexico, southern USA, this bank of radiotelescopes can probe deep into space. Thanks to instruments like these, we know far more about the universe than people did 50 years ago, and we have surveyed the entire solar system in amazing detail. But despite these extraordinary advances, technology has failed to solve many of the problems that we face back home on earth.

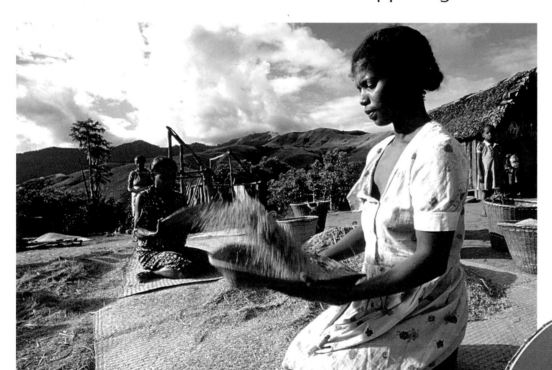

◀ In Madagascar, as in other developing countries, most people still depend directly on farming for their living. This woman is winnowing rice – a task that separates the edible grain from the unwanted husks. Over the centuries, Madagascar's farmers have transformed their island home, clearing forest and replacing it with a patchwork of pasture and fields. It is a change that has happened in many other parts of the world.

The agricultural revolution

For most of human history, people lived by hunting and by collecting food from the wild. To find enough to eat, they had to keep on the move. But roughly 10,000 years ago, a new kind of lifestyle began to appear as people discovered how to grow crops and keep animals for food. Farming meant that they could settle down in one place, and it generated surplus food that could be stored and traded. This revolutionary way of life had some far-reaching effects. It allowed towns and cities to develop, and it also transformed the countryside around them. With a more reliable food supply, the human population started to grow.

▶ During the 1800s, railways enabled people to travel farther and faster than they had ever done before. This photograph, taken in the Cascade Range mountains, USA, in 1885, shows a railway construction team posing proudly on a new wooden viaduct.

The industrial revolution

The second great revolution began when engineers discovered how to produce power from fuels, such as wood and coal. In the early 1700s, steam engines were used to operate the first factories and, later on, steam locomotives took to the rails. In the 20th century, the petrol-driven engine made power even easier to use. These engineering breakthroughs meant that people no longer had to rely on muscle power to get things done – machines could be used instead. Industrialization had many positive results, including progress in medicine and public health. But it also had some drawbacks. One of the most serious was the growth of pollution – a problem that is still with us today.

The information revolution

In 1946, US scientists tested the world's first all-purpose digital computer – a device that weighed over 30 tonnes. Called ENIAC, it heralded the start of the information revolution, which has transformed human life in little over 50 years. Thanks to computers, digital cameras and satellites, we can explore the remotest parts of the earth and the most distant corners of space, and we can monitor the health of our planet in a way that was not possible before. This kind of research highlights the problems caused by human beings, and the information it provides can also help us to reduce our impact on the natural world.

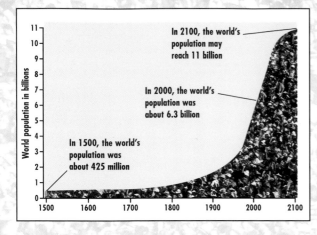

▲ This graph shows how the world's population has grown in the last 500 years, and it also looks forwards to the start of the 22nd century. At some point in the future, the population will stop growing, but no one knows for certain when.

Population growth

Every day, the world's population grows by about 200,000 people. There are now over three times as many people as there were a century ago, and today's figure could double by 2100. This increase is mainly due to progress in public health, which means that more people survive childhood to have children themselves. For the human species, it is an astonishing achievement, but our booming population creates problems for us, and for the rest of the living world.

Take-off

Until the late 1700s, the human population grew slowly, because many people died from diseases such as smallpox. But after the discovery of vaccination and improvements in sanitation, childhood deaths fell dramatically and the population began to boom. This burst of growth began in the industrialized countries of North America and western Europe, and from there it spread across the world.

▼ A Kenyan boy is vaccinated against diphtheria, polio and tetanus – diseases that once killed millions of children around the world. Like many developing countries, Kenya's population is booming thanks to better medical care.

Making the transition

The world's population is rising, but there are big differences in population growth across the globe. In many European countries, women have an average of less than two children, which is the number needed to keep the population steady. The population of these countries will fall unless extra people arrive from outside. In many African nations, however, the average is over five children, so the population is climbing sharply here. But Europe was once like this too. Through a process called the demographic transition, European family sizes have shrunk. Experts predict that, sooner or later, developing countries will experience this transition as well.

Closing the gap

In Europe and North America, the demographic transition took several generations to complete. But in some of today's developing countries, birth control programmes have helped to speed it up. India, for example, launched family planning in the 1950s, while China adopted a policy of one child per family in 1979. These measures are controversial, particularly when they involve tough penalties for breaking the rules. But they have had the desired effect. Without them, countries such as China would have millions of extra people to feed.

◀ A Chinese billboard from the 1980s explains the benefits of having just one child in each family. Over 20 years, this drastic population control policy reduced the number of births by about 230 million — almost four times the entire population of Great Britain.

一对夫妇只生育一个孩

少生

少生有利于国家,有利于家庭,有利于母亲与儿童

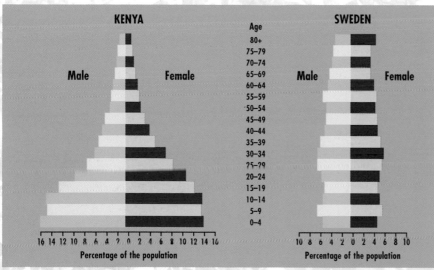

KENYA

Male   Female

SWEDEN

Male   Female

Age
80+
75–79
70–74
65–69
60–64
55–59
50–54
45–49
40–44
35–39
30–34
25–29
20–24
15–19
10–14
5–9
0–4

16 14 12 10 8 6 4 2 0 2 4 6 8 10 12 14 16
Percentage of the population

10 8 6 4 2 0 2 4 6 8 10
Percentage of the population

▲ This 'age pyramid' divides up Kenya's population according to people's ages. Young people are much more numerous than old people — a sign that the population is booming.

▲ Sweden's age pyramid looks quite different from Kenya's. The age groups are more or less balanced, showing that the population is stable. In Sweden, far more people survive into their seventies and eighties.

Joining the ranks

Thirty years ago, many scientists believed that the human population was running out of control. Looking forwards to the year 2000, some foresaw grim prospects for an overloaded earth. Their predictions have not come true, but our planet is certainly feeling the strain. Many environmental problems are directly linked to population, so the more of us there are, the harder they are to prevent. The good news is that human numbers look as though they will eventually reach a peak, and after that, they may even fall. The bad news is that all the extra people will want food, space and consumer goods, piling up further problems for the natural world.

Habitat destruction

The more people there are on earth, the more land they need. This simple fact lies at the heart of habitat destruction, a worldwide problem that is eating away at the natural world. Some habitats are destroyed to make way for farmland, while others are buried by buildings or roads. The quest for resources also damages habitats – particularly when it involves timber, minerals or oil.

Quarrying and mining

Bricks, concrete, windows and drink cans have one thing in common – they are all produced by quarrying or mining. So is coal, as well as the crushed stone that is used to build roads. Life without these materials would be hard, but getting hold of them can have damaging effects on the living world. Quarries and mines obliterate habitats – either by digging them up, or by smothering them under piles of waste.

Vanishing wetlands

Beneath swamps and salt marshes are some of the most fertile soils on earth. This helps to explain why so many of the world's wetlands have been drained and turned into fields. In the USA, over half the nation's wetlands have disappeared since 1800, and the remainder is shrinking fast. Healthy wetlands play a useful role in controlling floods and purifying water, and they are rich in wildlife. But when wetlands vanish, their wildlife disappears as well.

Lake Okeechobee

ATLANTIC OCEAN

SOUTHERN FLORIDA

Miami

GULF OF MEXICO

KEY TO MAP

Permanently flooded land, 1900

Permanently flooded land, today

◀ ▼ The Florida Everglades, in southeastern USA, are the wetland home of more than a dozen endangered species of animals, including the snail kite and the American crocodile. Before humans began to drain them, the Everglades were like a huge sheet of water flowing gently towards the sea. Today, canals and pipelines divert much of this water to farms and towns, and only isolated pockets of swamp stay flooded all year round.

▲ Healthy coral reefs (left) teem with life, making them perfect places
for fishing. But when fishermen use dynamite to stun their catch, the coral
is often killed. With the coral dead, the reef soon disintegrates (right).

Damage offshore

Land habitats have always been hit hardest by our
need for space and food. But in the last 50 years,
habitat destruction has also spread offshore. Fishing
boats trawl their nets over the seabed, scraping up
plants and animals, and creating long-lasting scars.
Coral reefs are affected by overfishing, and by
sediment that is washed off the land – particularly
from towns and farms. An even more serious
problem is global warming, which can make coral
sicken and die. Faced with all these threats, many
of the world's coral reefs are already in trouble.

Deforestation

Forests are the richest habitats on land, and also some of
the most threatened. Since farming began, over half the
world's tree cover has been cleared to make way for fields.
In some places – such as Europe – deforestation took place
long ago, but in the tropics it began far more recently,
and is happening at record-breaking speed. Tropical
forests are cleared for farms, and also for their timber:
a single trunk can be worth as much as 5,000 US dollars.

The loss of tropical forests is a disaster for wildlife.
Over a third of the world's birds rely on this habitat for
survival, together with two-thirds of all primates – animals
that include monkeys and apes. Tropical forests are also
the natural home of about half of the world's broadleaved
trees. As forests become smaller and are divided up by
roads, all these species face a tough fight for survival.

◀ The Bingham Canyon copper mine, in Utah, USA, is the largest in
the world. In giant mines like this, the metal content of the rock is often
as low as five per cent. For every kilogram of metal that is recovered,
19kg of polluting waste has to be dug up, processed and dumped.

Growing food

Farmland is essential for our survival. Today's crops yield much better harvests than ones 50 years ago, but with a growing population, the pressure is on to produce even more. This is a tough challenge, because farmland needs to be kept in good condition so that it can keep producing food year after year. If things go wrong, the results can be disastrous: crops can fail, and the soil may even disappear.

Intensive farming

To produce good yields, crops need fertile soil. Traditionally, farmers fertilized soil by adding animal manure – a technique that organic farmers still use today. But in 1909, Fritz Haber, a German chemist, devised a way of making artificial fertilizer. Haber's invention launched intensive farming – a type of agriculture that relies on artificial inputs, such as fertilizers, pesticides, fuel and animal feed. Intensive farming has increased world food production dramatically, but at a price: it uses a lot of energy, and its chemicals often contaminate soil, water and food.

◀ During the 'dustbowl' years, in the 1930s, billions of tonnes of soil blew off farmland in midwestern USA. This ecological disaster was created by drought and poor farming practices. In some parts of the world today, soil is disappearing more than 10,000 times faster than it is being made.

Soil erosion

In natural habitats, the remains of dead plants break down to form soil, and the roots of living plants hold the soil in place. But when the ground is cleared and ploughed, the soil can be washed away by rain or blown away by wind. Soil erosion is a big problem for farmers, because new soil forms very slowly – often at a rate of less than 1mm a year.

▲ About a third of the world's land surface is used for farming. Here, an intensively farmed field of maize is being harvested to make animal feed.

▶ Planes swoop over a field in Texas, southern USA, dusting a crop with pesticides. Each field may be treated with over a dozen different chemicals before the crop is ready to be harvested.

Farming and wildlife

Until the 1950s, fields often teemed with colourful weeds, and farmland birds could rely on plentiful seeds and insects. Some organic farms are still like this, but intensive farmland is very different. Herbicides and pesticides keep weeds and insects at bay, while combine harvesters gather up every speck of grain. Hedges and trees are cleared away to make larger fields, leaving wild animals with nowhere to breed. These changes help farms produce food more efficiently, with fewer losses from pests and disease. The downside is that wild plants and animals find themselves squeezed out.

Feeding the world

Despite the surge in the human population, the world's farmland still produces enough food to keep everyone on the planet properly fed. This has been achieved by clearing more land, by making farming more intensive, and by breeding better strains of crops. Even so, three-quarters of the world's people – mainly in Africa and Asia – have less food than they need. The reason is that food supplies are unevenly spread. Developed regions, such as North America and Europe, produce more food than they can consume, while poorer parts of the world go short. Here, farmers do not have the money to buy improved seed and tools, and climatic hazards – such as droughts and floods – often make a difficult situation worse. Emergency food aid can prevent people starving, but the real solution to hunger is to help farmers get the most from their land.

▼ These hungry children are eating a much-needed meal at a relief centre in Somalia. In this part of eastern Africa, a long civil war has made it difficult for farmers to grow food.

Expanding cities

If you live in North America or Europe, there is a 75 per cent chance that your home is in a town or city, rather than in the countryside. If you live in Australia or Japan, the likelihood is bigger still. In the near future, over half the world's population will live in urban surroundings – an enormous change from the days when most people's homes were on or near to farmland. Urban living has a huge impact on the natural world, because almost everything that people need has to be brought in from outside.

Cities and megacities
In 1800, just one city in the world – Beijing, in China – had more than one million inhabitants. At that time, most people had never been to a city, and they had no real idea of what urban life was like. Since then, the world's cities have grown at an amazing rate. China alone has over 70 cities with a million-plus people, and the world's largest cities have shot past the 15 million mark. These 'megacities' include São Paulo, Mumbai and Tokyo, which sprawl over hundreds of square kilometres of land. Each one is swelling by thousands of people a day, so counting their population is an almost impossible task.

▲ Mexico City is home to almost 21 million people. With around three million cars, the city's traffic jams are notorious, and air pollution is a serious health hazard.

Why cities grow
Because the human population is rising fast, cities grow too. But another change is also fuelling urban growth. Before the industrial revolution (see page 21), most people worked on the land, and in the least developed countries, many still do. But when countries become industrialized, there are more jobs in cities than in the countryside, and people begin to move. This is happening in China, southern Asia and Latin America – three regions with the fastest-growing cities in the world.

▼ Most people dream of owning their own home. This picture, taken in Texas, southern USA, shows what happens when the dream comes true: wide belts of newly built houses spread across the countryside.

▶ Mumbai, or Bombay, is the largest city in India, and also its leading port. It is a place of stark contrasts, with a thriving commercial centre and luxury hotels, but also shanty towns made up of rough, home-made shacks that let in the monsoon rains.

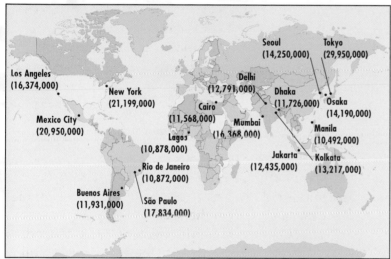

Seoul (14,250,000)
Tokyo (29,950,000)
Los Angeles (16,374,000)
Delhi (12,791,000)
New York (21,199,000)
Dhaka (11,726,000)
Cairo (11,568,000)
Osaka (14,190,000)
Mexico City (20,950,000)
Mumbai (16,368,000)
Lagos (10,878,000)
Manila (10,492,000)
Jakarta (12,435,000)
Kolkata (13,217,000)
Rio de Janeiro (10,872,000)
Buenos Aires (11,931,000)
São Paulo (17,834,000)

▲ In the year 2002, 17 cities had populations of more than ten million people. In developing countries, most cities are still growing quickly, but in North America and western Europe, many have stopped expanding because people have started to move to smaller towns.

Living on the edge

When a city's population grows gradually, houses and services can be planned in advance. But in many developing nations, resources are scarce and housing can be hard to find. So the poorest city-dwellers are forced to build their own homes from whatever they can find. On the outskirts of cities such as Rio de Janeiro, Cape Town and Mumbai, makeshift houses are crowded together in 'shanty towns'. Life here can be extremely tough. Few shanty towns have a proper water supply or sanitation, and good jobs are rare.

Spreading suburbs

Unplanned housing often causes environmental problems, but so does housing in more prosperous parts of the world. Here, suburban housing estates spread into the countryside, destroying natural habitats. Because these houses each have their own garage and garden, they take up far more space than city-centre homes. Spreading suburbs are a problem in crowded countries, such as Britain, but they are also a headache in North America and Australia – places famous for their wide-open spaces. In the USA, new suburbs swallow up nearly 10,000km² of land each year, or 12 times the area of central New York City.

The age of waste

▲ This overflowing bin shows one of the reasons why we produce so much waste: food and drink are sold in packages designed to be thrown away.

The next time you buy a takeaway meal, think about what happens to the packaging. It is used just once, but its lifetime may be as long as your own. Waste like this adds to the vast mountain of rubbish that each of us throws away every year. Today, waste is a global problem – one that reaches even the remotest parts of the world.

▲ Many of the world's beaches are littered with waste, even though it is illegal for ships to dump rubbish at sea.

Changes in the bin

Human lifestyles have altered a lot in the last century, and our rubbish has changed as well. In 1900, there was very little packaging, and major purchases were built to last. Nowadays, packaging is everywhere, and the things we buy – from clothes to mobile phones – soon become out-of-date or obsolete. In a world where shopping has become a major pastime, each of us generates up to a tonne of household waste every year.

Getting rid of waste

Modern-day rubbish contains large amounts of plastics – man-made materials that are very resistant to decay. Plastics are extremely useful, and it is hard to imagine life without them. But because bacteria and other microbes cannot break them down, they never quite disappear. Plastic objects often tear apart, but the fragments that are left behind can last for hundreds of years.

Besides plastics, household and industrial waste contains countless different materials, all jumbled together. Disposing of it safely is not easy. The traditional solution – burying it in landfill sites – causes problems, because rubbish decomposes underground. It can give off hazardous gases, and liquids that can trickle into rivers. An alternative is to burn it in special incinerators; the heat can even be used to generate electric power. But incinerators are controversial, because they release dangerous pollutants into the air.

Rubbish at sea

Seawater is always on the move, so it spreads rubbish far and wide. Waste can drift across oceans, and even remote islands collect rubbish on their shores. In the 1990s, a beach survey was carried out on Ducie Island, which is uninhabited by humans. Despite being one of the world's most isolated spots, 4,500km from the coast of South America, hundreds of pieces of rubbish were found, from plastic toys to gas cylinders. Drifting waste is not just an eyesore – it is a menace to sea animals. Ropes and nets can entangle seals and birds, both at sea and on the shore. Plastic bags may be swallowed by turtles and porpoises, which mistake them for jellyfish, their normal prey.

◄ After scavenging at a rubbish dump, this white stork has become tangled in a plastic bag. Unless it can free itself, the stork's chances of survival are slim.

Waste and wildlife

Humans do not find rubbish attractive, which is why we usually hide it out of sight. But for many animals, domestic waste holds the irresistible promise of food. Birds flock to landfill sites all over the world, and on city streets, plastic rubbish bags attract nocturnal scavengers, such as foxes and raccoons. In Churchill, northern Canada, one waste site has even become a magnet for polar bears – repeat offenders have to be caught and removed by helicopter to prevent them becoming a danger near the town. None of these animals can help its behaviour, because nature has shaped them to eat whatever they find. But animals and human rubbish are a dangerous mixture. Scavengers can drag away waste, scattering it and causing a health hazard. The animals are also at risk themselves, because rubbish is full of dangerous objects that can injure or even kill them.

▼ With so much waste to deal with, landfills can reach an amazing size. Before it closed, New York's main site, on Staten Island, covered almost 900 hectares (equal to about 1,250 football fields), with mounds up to 60m high.

Liquid assets

Water is one resource that everybody needs. But one in five people do not have access to safe drinking water, and in some parts of the world, freshwater is becoming increasingly scarce. To make matters more complicated, water is often used as a cheap and easy way to dispose of waste. Water pollution creates problems for people, and also for anything else living downstream.

▼ Industrial pollution kills water life, and can contaminate drinking water supplies. The water gushing out of this pipe is obviously polluted, but some other kinds of water pollution are much harder to spot.

▼ Clean water is vital for good health. This Kenyan boy has access to clean water close to his home, but many people in developing countries have to use unsafe water, and they may face a long walk to fetch it.

Water on tap

Few of us stop to think about where water comes from when we turn on the tap. In places with a damp climate, household water is usually drawn from rivers or lakes. Sometimes, this surface water is piped hundreds of kilometres to places that are normally dry. But in most dry regions, such as Australia and midwestern USA, water comes mainly from boreholes and wells. This underground water trickles through microscopic spaces deep in the rocks, and it moves so slowly that it can be thousands of years old. Groundwater is a highly valuable resource but, like many others, it is being used a lot faster than it is being replaced.

A growing thirst

To stay alive, the average person needs less than four litres of water a day, unless the climate is very hot. But where water is available at the turn of a tap, most people get through much more than this. Americans top the list, using about 230 litres per day, while people in Europe and Japan are not far behind. But personal water consumption is only part of the story, because farms and factories use water on a massive scale. When this is included as well, the amount of water used per person often jumps by over ten times.

When more means less

Our thirst for water can have a big impact on the natural world. One of Europe's largest wetlands, the Coto de Doñana, in southern Spain, has shrunk by four-fifths because so much water is used for irrigation. And under the North American Great Plains, one of the world's largest groundwater deposits, or aquifers, is shrinking fast for the same reason. Some experts think that it will be exhausted by 2040, leaving a vitally important grain-growing region running on an empty tank.

Water pollution

Water is good at dissolving things, which makes it ideal for disposing of waste. But if waste water contaminates drinking supplies, all sorts of health problems can follow. In developed countries, drinking water is often purified and sewage is processed to reduce the chance of pollution. But this is an expensive job that many poorer countries cannot afford. As a result, about a billion people are forced to drink unsafe water, and at least five million people die each year from waterborne diseases. Wild animals also suffer, particularly when water is polluted by chemicals from factories and farmland.

Unfair shares

In dry parts of the world, water can be a source of friction – particularly when someone takes more than their share. During the 1960s, for example, the government of the Soviet Union began a huge irrigation programme in central Asia, using water that flowed into the Aral Sea. Today, the Aral Sea has shrunk by more than half, leaving fishing boats high and dry. In the Middle East, tension over water could have even more dangerous results. This region is desperately short of water, and its countries need more each year. If agreement is not reached, the result could be a water war.

▲ Lake Powell is one of several artificial reservoirs on the Colorado river, in southwestern USA. So much water is withdrawn from these lakes – for use on farms and in cities – that the river sometimes dries up before it reaches the sea.

▼ A rusting fishing boat lies stranded on the dried-up shore of the Aral Sea. Four decades after its water started to be diverted for irrigation, this inland sea has been declared an ecological disaster zone.

Litres per person per day

This chart shows the average daily water consumption per person per day in all the inhabited continents. The figures include household use, agricultural use and also industrial use.

3,500
3,000
2,500
2,000
1,500
1,000
500
0

North America | South America | Europe | Africa | Asia | Australasia

Energy addicts

Over the last two centuries, the world's population has used more energy than the whole human race did in the previous 50,000 years. For most of us, life becomes difficult if the electricity goes off, so it is hard to imagine what it would be like if we ran out of energy and the power never came back on. Fortunately, this is unlikely to happen, but our spiralling need for energy creates environmental problems that are proving difficult to solve. For a world addicted to energy, this means some tricky choices now, and in the years to come.

▼ Each year, the world gets through more than three billion tonnes of oil. Producing this much oil is a huge and complicated operation, involving oilfields on land and offshore. This drilling rig stands off the north coast of Alaska; in the shallow waters of the icy Beaufort Sea.

The big burn

Animals need energy to live, and they produce it from their food. But long ago, humans learned how to release extra energy by setting things alight. At first, this energy would have been difficult to use, but people gradually developed the technology to put it to work. Today, energy keeps us warm, it carries information in computers and mobile phones, and it powers aircraft as they criss-cross the skies. There are many ways of getting energy, but for most of our needs we still rely on the age-old method of setting things on fire.

Fossil fuels

▼ During the 1970s, two massive oil price rises triggered shortages and power cuts all over the western world. Three decades later, the lights are on full again, and we are burning up oil faster than ever before.

Wood is an important fuel in the developing world, but industrialized countries rely mainly on coal, natural gas and oil. These are known as fossil fuels, because they formed from the remains of plants that lived millions of years ago. These plants collected energy from sunlight, and the energy they stored is released when fossil fuels are burned. Coal supplies about a quarter of the world's energy, and natural gas about a fifth. Oil comes out top, at about 40 per cent, because it is so convenient for powering things that move.

How long will fossil fuels last?

Of all the fossil fuels, coal is the only one that is not in danger of running out. The earth still contains billions of tonnes in unused coal reserves, which could last over 500 years. Unfortunately, coal has many drawbacks as a fuel. It is difficult to dig, expensive to distribute, and it creates serious air pollution when it is burned. Natural gas is much cleaner, which is why many power stations have switched from coal to gas. There is a lot less of it, however, so today's 'dash for gas' is unlikely to last for long. With oil, the future is complicated. New oil deposits are discovered every year, and new ways are found of getting the most out of existing oilfields. But even so, many experts think that we are nearing the peak of oil production, and that we will soon be heading for a decline. By the year 2050, oil will still be available, but it may well be scarce. This means it could be far too expensive for many of the things we use it for today.

▲ Chernobyl nuclear power station lies in ruins after a catastrophic explosion in April 1986. More than 200,000 people had to be evacuated from their homes – many have not been able to return.

NATURAL GAS
World reserves: 120 billion tonnes
Rate of use: 1.9 billion tonnes per year
Time to depletion: about 60 years

OIL
World reserves: 140 billion tonnes
Rate of use: 3.2 billion tonnes per year
Time to depletion: about 45 years

COAL
World reserves: 1,200 billion tonnes
Rate of use: 2.2 billion tonnes per year
Time to depletion: about 550 years

◄ This chart shows current reserves of the three fossil fuels, together with estimates of how long they are likely to last. Reserves sometimes go up when new deposits are found, but they can never be used completely. That is because the costs of extraction leap upwards as a fuel becomes more scarce.

The nuclear solution?

In the 1950s, the USA, Britain and France began to generate electricity by nuclear power. Unlike fossil fuels, the uranium fuel used in nuclear power stations does not burn. Instead, its atoms split apart into lighter ones, releasing a colossal amount of energy. A coal-burning power station uses several tonnes of fuel a minute, but a nuclear power station can run on less than one tonne of uranium a week. With this incredible potential, nuclear power once seemed to be the answer to the world's energy problems. Today, we know differently. Because uranium fuel is highly radioactive, nuclear power stations need strict safety measures, and this makes them very expensive to build and to maintain. Even so, there have been a number of accidents – the worst, in the Ukrainian town of Chernobyl in 1986, created a radioactive cloud that covered a large part of Europe. This single disaster persuaded many governments that nuclear power is not worth the risk.

Air pollution

Water pollution is an age-old problem, but air pollution really got under way when people started to burn fossil fuels. Eventually, city air became so bad that many countries had to tackle it by law: Britain passed a Clean Air Act in 1956, and the USA did the same in 1963. These measures helped a lot, but air pollution has not gone away.

▼ After a century in polluted air, this statue is being dissolved by acid rain. Acid rain attacks anything made of marble or limestone, and it can also corrode metals and bleach the colour from paint. In cities and towns, it causes damage costing billions of dollars a year.

Blowing in the wind

Unlike water, air is everywhere, and there is no danger of it running out. But fresh air is a different matter. Indoor air is often full of dust and man-made chemicals, while outdoor air contains gases and microscopic particles from factories, power stations and vehicle exhausts. Some pollutants do not travel far, because they soon settle to the ground. Others can spread hundreds of kilometres downwind, affecting people and wildlife. A few stay in the atmosphere for many years – long enough for them to spread all over the earth.

Acid rain

In the 1980s, strange things started happening in the forests of central Europe. Trees lost their leaves, and thousands of them slowly died. German scientists called it *Waldsterben*, or 'forest death', and thought that it might be a new plant disease. But then a different culprit came to light, called acid rain. Acid rain is produced when gases in smoke dissolve in droplets of airborne moisture. It looks and feels quite harmless, but it can kill trees and fish, and even eat through stone. Today, acid rain affects many countries. Tall chimneys spread the problem, so the countryside is sometimes hit worse than places close to cities or towns.

▶ This colour-coded satellite map shows the ozone hole as a ragged, dark-blue ring above Antarctica. On New Zealand's South Island, and near the tip of South America, the thin ozone layer makes it easy to be sunburned, even on cloudy days.

◀ Around large cities, pollution soars during the rush hour, when nose-to-tail cars pump exhaust fumes into the air. Many cities now use automatic ozone detectors to track pollution levels and to warn people when it would be better not to drive.

The ozone hole

Ozone is one of the worst ingredients of photochemical smog, because it attacks living cells. But much higher up in the atmosphere, a layer of natural ozone protects us against harmful radiation from the sun. This vital shield, between 20km and 45km high, has been in place for millions of years. But in the early 1980s, scientists discovered that the layer seemed to thin and then disappear over Antarctica during the southern winter. Some years later, thinning was found over the north pole too.

We depend on the ozone layer, so this discovery was extremely serious news. Remarkably, it had been predicted over ten years earlier by two US scientists, Mario Molina and Sherwood Rowland. They found that high-level ozone could be destroyed by chemicals called chlorofluorocarbons, or CFCs. At the time, CFCs were widely used in aerosols, refrigerators and plastics, and large amounts escaped into the air. Once airborne, CFCs drift up into the ozone layer. Here, they break down ozone molecules, and they keep doing it for many years. The world's reaction to this crisis was unusually fast and effective (see page 48). Today, the ozone hole is still with us, but it shows signs of being on the mend. Impressively, by 2040 it may have finally closed.

Cars and smog

Car exhaust fumes contribute to acid rain, and they also contain poisonous gases, such as carbon monoxide and ozone, and tiny particles of soot which can travel deep into our lungs. Exhaust pollution is worst in cities that have lots of traffic and where the climate is often sunny and calm, such as Los Angeles, USA. In these conditions, the sunshine triggers off chemical reactions, creating a murky brown layer known as photochemical smog. The smog is poisonous to plants, and it irritates people's eyes and lungs. It can be reduced by making cars burn fuel more cleanly, but with so many cars on the roads, it is hard to bring under control.

▼ Smoke from power stations and heavy industries contains sulphur dioxide, the chief cause of acid rain. In the air, this gas forms tiny droplets of sulphuric acid — the same substance found in car batteries.

The greenhouse effect

If you get into a car that has been parked in the sunshine, the temperature inside is often much higher than outside. This is just one example of the greenhouse effect, something that is essential for life on earth. The greenhouse effect keeps our planet warm – without it, most of the surface would be frozen solid. In recent years, air pollution has increased the greenhouse effect, making the earth's temperature rise. If it continues, this worldwide change could be the biggest one ever caused by human beings.

▲ Heated by sunshine, mist rises over a lake and vaporizes into the air. Water vapour is the most important greenhouse gas. If the world continues to warm up, there could be a lot more of it in the air – something that would make the earth warmer still.

▼ The atmosphere is like an insulating jacket wrapped around the earth. Because it traps heat, it warms the planet's surface by more than 30°C. Without it, life would only be possible in the tropics, and most of the world's water would be frozen solid.

How the greenhouse effect works

When sunlight reaches the earth, some of it is reflected back into space, but most of it travels through the atmosphere until it hits the planet's surface. Here, it warms up the land and the oceans, making the earth give off energy in return. This outgoing energy is quite different from sunlight. It has a long wavelength, which makes it invisible, and it is given off from the whole of the earth's surface 24 hours a day. Unlike sunlight, this energy can be absorbed by some of the gases that are found in air. This difference is crucial, because it means that outgoing energy finds it harder to escape into space. As a result, the earth clings on to its heat, staying warmer than it would otherwise be.

▶ These two diagrams show how the greenhouse effect works, and what happens when extra greenhouse gases build up in the air. With a stable greenhouse gas layer (diagram A), the planet collects heat from sunshine, but at the same time it loses energy through long-wave radiation that travels into space. If greenhouse gases increase (diagram B), this balance changes. Less long-wave radiation escapes, so the planet keeps gaining energy. As a result, it warms up.

Energy in sunlight passes through the atmosphere

Long-wave radiation carries energy back into space

Stable greenhouse gases

Greenhouse gases block some of the outgoing radiation

Earth's surface warms up

A

► Car engines give off a mixture of greenhouse gases, including carbon dioxide and nitrous oxide. Carbon dioxide plays a key part in the greenhouse effect. It is a natural part of the atmosphere, but humans have released billions of extra tonnes by burning fossil fuels.

◄ Humans have created some greenhouse gases – such as CFCs, or chlorofluorocarbons – that did not exist on earth before. Until the 1980s, CFCs were used as coolants in refrigerators. These powerful greenhouse gases were phased out after the discovery of the ozone hole, and levels in the atmosphere have recently started to fall.

Greenhouse gases

Our nearest neighbour, the Moon, does not have an atmosphere, and its night-time temperature can plunge to –170°C. But back on earth, the atmosphere and its greenhouse gases keep conditions comfortable for life. Water vapour accounts for about two-thirds of the greenhouse effect. The remaining third is produced by carbon dioxide, methane, nitrous oxide and man-made CFCs (see page 37). Since 1750, humans have increased the carbon dioxide level by nearly a third, because it is given off when fossil fuels are burned. We have also stepped up the levels of all the other greenhouse gases.

A changing balance

With greenhouse gas levels on the rise, the greenhouse effect is increasing too. Most scientists believe this is why the earth's surface is warming up – a disturbing development that you can read about over the page. So far, global warming has been slight, but two uncomfortable facts mean that we face a lot more in the future. Firstly, most greenhouse gases are an inevitable side effect of the way we live. If we want to reduce them, we will have to change. Secondly, some greenhouse gases are very long-lived. Even if we stop releasing them now, they will remain overhead for years to come.

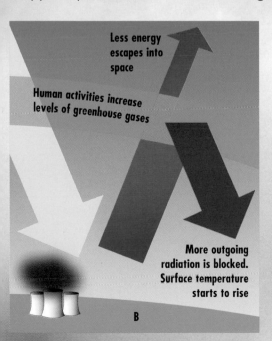

Less energy escapes into space

Human activities increase levels of greenhouse gases

More outgoing radiation is blocked. Surface temperature starts to rise

B

► Rice terraces, seen here on the Indonesian island of Bali, are a source of methane – a powerful greenhouse gas. Methane is released whenever anything rots down in stagnant water, and it is also given off by grazing mammals. During the last 250 years, the atmosphere's methane level has doubled. The construction of reservoirs and the growth of farming are mainly to blame.

Climate change

In 2003, forest fires raged throughout Europe as the
continent experienced its warmest summer on record.
In 1998, the entire world recorded its warmest year for at least
a century, and perhaps for over a thousand years. Figures like these
fit a disturbing trend – one that has almost certainly been triggered
by the human race. By polluting the atmosphere, we have strengthened
the greenhouse effect, and rising temperatures are the result. In the
coming century, climate change will have far-reaching effects – for us,
for our food supply, and for the whole of the natural world.

▲ In southern Europe,
a pine forest is swallowed up
during the fires of 2003. As
the world warms up, disasters
like this are likely to happen
more often, threatening
houses, people and wildlife.

KEY TO MAP

| -2°C | -1°C | 0°C | +1°C | +2°C | +3°C | +4°C | +5°C |

Temperature change

▲ According to IPCC predictions, the world's average surface temperature could rise
by up to 5°C over the course of the coming century. This map shows the temperature
change expected by 2050, during the winter months in the northern hemisphere.

Patterns in the past

Climate change is almost as old as the earth itself. In the
past, ice ages have plunged the planet into a long-lasting
freeze, while periods called interglacials have brought much
warmer conditions – the last one started about 10,000
years ago, and is continuing today. Up to a point, warm
conditions are good, because they encourage plants to
grow. But too much warmth can have very damaging
effects, particularly if the change is fast. That kind of change
is exactly what most scientists think we are seeing today.

Who is to blame?

Natural climate change is caused by many factors, which
means that it impossible to predict. This, in turn, makes
it very difficult to decide if human activities are playing
a part. A small minority of scientists believe that today's
global warming is just a hiccup that will soon reverse.
Others think that it is significant, but they do not believe
that human activities are the cause. But most experts
strongly disagree. According to the Intergovernmental
Panel on Climate Change (IPCC), global warming is
happening now, and humans are to blame.

◀ In a warmer world, crop failures from drought will be more common.

Cause and effects

If you live in a region that has a cool climate, global warming might sound like a good thing. But a steep rise in the earth's surface temperature could make life difficult in many ways. Some parts of the world will become hotter and drier, including regions that supply much of the world's food. With more heat energy in the atmosphere and in the oceans, other areas could be hit by powerful hurricanes and typhoons. In a warmer world, polar ice will melt and seawater will expand. In the next century, this could raise the sea level by almost 1m, flooding low-lying coasts and islands. These changes will be difficult enough for people, but for many plants and animals they could be disastrous.

To reverse global warming, we will have to reduce the amount of greenhouse gases that we release. This is an immense challenge and, as you can find out in chapter 3, there are a lot of ideas – and disagreements – about how this should be done.

▲ Coral islands are often just a few metres above sea level, putting them in the firing line from global warming. Some island states – such as Tuvalu in the Pacific Ocean – have threatened to sue countries that do not control their output of greenhouse gases.

Wildlife under threat

Because living things evolve, they are able to adapt to gradual changes in the world around them. Evolution is a slow process, however – much too slow for animals and plants to keep up with today's rapidly changing world. As a result, a record number of species are finding it very difficult to survive.

Changing times

A hundred years ago, most people believed that wildlife existed to be exploited, whatever and wherever it was. Animals were hunted without any thought to conservation, and some species were pushed to the edge of extinction. In 1911, George V – the British king – took part in a hunt in India that killed 39 tigers over just 11 days. Fortunately, attitudes have changed, and fewer people support this kind of careless persecution. But even so, thousands of species are already on the endangered list, simply because they share the planet with us.

◄ The bittern – a kind of heron that lives in reedbeds – is a typical casualty of the changing world. Centuries ago, it was hunted for food, but today it is threatened far more by the disappearance of its natural habitat.

▼ The fight to save the tiger is one of the great conservation challenges. Tigers are under threat from habitat destruction and the illegal trade in their body parts, which are used in oriental medicines.

Deadly competitors

Some of the worst accidental damage to wildlife has been caused by animals and plants that humans have spread around the world. This may sound harmless, but in isolated places, introduced species can drive native ones into extinction. For example, New Zealand's birds have been decimated by European mammals, while Hawaii's wildlife has been swamped by animals and plants from five continents. The result is that a limited number of successful species now crop up all over the world.

As well as introduced species, wild plants and animals have to deal with human beings. As our population grows, natural habitats shrink, leaving less room for the natural world. Small animals can often survive in small patches of ground, but for large ones, from tigers to giant pandas, shortage of living space can be a deadly threat.

Wildlife in a warmer world

In recent years, conservationists have had some spectacular successes in rescuing endangered species – you can find out about some of them on pages 54–55. But in the 21st century, wildlife faces a new menace that will be very difficult to control. This threat is global warming and, unlike hunting or habitat loss, it could affect the majority of species on earth.

For scientists, the warmer world is still new territory, and no one knows quite how well, or badly, the planet's animals and plants will cope. But some recent projections, published by a panel of scientists in 2004, make alarming reading. The team studied six of the world's richest wildlife regions, and used computers to predict how more than 1,000 different species would fare. They found that by 2050, between 15 and 37 per cent of them would no longer exist.

▲ Overcollection and habitat destruction threaten many of the world's flowering plants, particularly tropical orchids. More than 5,000 species of flowering plants are listed as being endangered, but the figure is certain to rise as scientists carry out more research.

Winners and losers

With something as complex as climate change, future predictions are often wrong. For example, when global warming was first detected, some scientists predicted an 8m rise in the sea level by the year 2100. Today, most experts think that this figure is a huge overestimate. But even if today's predictions are wildly out, and animals and plants do much better than expected, thousands of species are still likely to disappear. Global warming is already under way, and it cannot be stopped in a hurry. For many borderline species, human help could make the difference between survival and extinction.

▼ Polar bears need sea ice to hunt, because they attack seals when they come to the surface to breathe. In a warmer world, most of the Arctic Ocean could stay ice-free all winter, putting pressure on one of the world's largest carnivores.

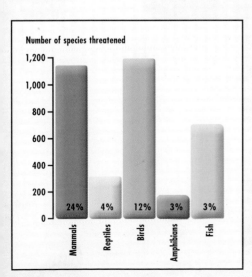

Number of species threatened

| | 1,200 |
| 1,000 |
| 800 |
| 600 |
| 400 |
| 200 |
| 0 |

24%   4%   12%   3%   3%

Mammals   Reptiles   Birds   Amphibians   Fish

◄ This chart shows the number of vertebrate species that are currently listed as critically endangered, endangered or vulnerable in the 2002 Red Data Lists. For example, almost 1,200 bird species are threatened, or 12 per cent of all bird species on earth. For fish in particular, these figures are only the tip of the iceberg, because many species have not yet been given a 'health check' by scientists. For more information on Red Data Lists, see page 44.

SUMMARY OF CHAPTER 2: PLANET UNDER PRESSURE

The people planet

This book began by exploring the living world, and the connections that keep it working. This chapter looked at something that is disturbing these connections: the ever-growing human race. Today, there are over six billion people on the planet, and the total is rising fast. Because we are so numerous, we have some kind of effect on almost every other species on earth. Thanks to us, an increasing number of them are finding it difficult to survive.

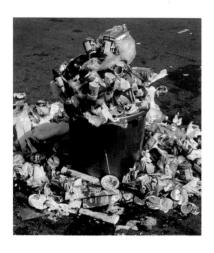

Most fast food packaging is designed to be used just once before being thrown away.

Disappearing habitats

To stay alive, the human population needs an immense supply of food. This is the main reason behind the wave of habitat destruction that has affected many parts of the world. Habitats are destroyed to make way for farmland, and to provide the raw materials and fuel that we use. They are also cleared to make way for towns, cities and roads. During the last 50 years, habitat clearance has accelerated as more people switch to an urban way of life.

Waste and global warming

Unlike people several generations ago, we live in a consumer age. Our modern lifestyles use a lot of energy, and almost all of it comes from fossil fuels: oil, coal and natural gas. As consumers, we generate ever-growing amounts of waste, from plastic packaging to the gases released by chimneys and car exhausts. Some of these gases damage the ozone layer, produce acid rain or trigger photochemical smog. Others are responsible for global warming – a change that will bring major problems for the living world. As the planet's surface warms by up to 5°C over the coming century, thousands of plant and animal species could become extinct.

Go further...

 Read the latest headlines at the UN Food and Agriculture Organization, an international agency helping to combat hunger around the world: www.fao.org/english/newsroom/action/index.html

Find out more about climate change and its effects by visiting the BBC Weather Centre: www.bbc.co.uk/climate

Discover more about endangered species by using the searchable Red List database created by the IUCN: www.redlist.org/search/search-basic.html

Global Warming by Fred Pearce (Dorling Kindersley, 2002)

 Agronomist
Studies farming techniques and food production.

Botanist
Studies plants and how they grow.

Climatologist
Examines the way that the climate works, and how it changes.

Demographer
Investigates population size, and the factors that make it rise or fall.

Hydrologist
Analyzes the world's water resources, on the surface and underground.

Zoologist
Studies animals and how they live.

 Visit one of the birthplaces of the industrial revolution by visiting the Ironbridge Gorge Museums, now classified as a World Heritage Site.
The Ironbridge Gorge Museums
Coach Road, Coalbrookdale
Shropshire TF8 7DQ, UK
Telephone: +44 (0) 1952 884391
www.ironbridge.org.uk/ironbridge/index.asp

Find out how one of the world's biggest cities has grown over the centuries by visiting the Museum of London.
Museum of London
London Wall
London EC2Y 5HN, UK
Telephone: +44 (0) 870 444 3852
www.museumoflondon.org.uk

CHAPTER 3

Sustainable world

Imagine that the earth is a business. Its future prospects do not look great: every year, its production lines work faster and faster, but its raw materials are dwindling at a frightening rate. In the drive to boost output, maintenance is often ignored, and the company's power and water supplies are under strain. This is a dangerous combination, and without urgent action the business looks bound to fail.

Far fetched? Perhaps. But in many ways, this is the world we live in today. For too long, people have treated the world just as they like, without worrying about the effects. But as we have seen in chapter 2, the past is catching up with us, and it is clear that things will have to change. In this chapter, you can read about what is being done to reduce our impact, so that planet earth can be nursed back to good health.

Eco-friendly, energy-efficient housing near Croydon, southern England

Conserving resources

Humans do not have a good track record at using the world's resources. All too often, we use them up in an uncontrolled rush, as everyone scrambles for a share. The result is environmental damage – sometimes on a massive scale. Fortunately, there are signs that the world is moving away from this 'grab-it-while-you-can' lifestyle.

▲ Whaling is a classic example of the misuse of the planet's resources, with several species being hunted to the very edge of extinction. At present, commercial whaling is suspended, but some countries are keen for it to restart.

Sustainable use

Many resources can be used just once, because they take so long to form. Oil is one example; another is the 'fossil' groundwater used to irrigate fields. Once these run out, it could take hundreds or even millions of human lifetimes for them to be replaced. But some resources are renewed all the time. These include living things and energy from the sun, and also everything that the sun powers, such as the wind and waves. Because the sun keeps delivering fresh supplies of energy, these resources can be harvested year after year. To create a sustainable world, we need to depend much more on resources like these. At the same time, we must limit the harvest of animals and plants, so that nature has time to replace what we use.

Action for change

One hundred years ago, lumberjacks were cutting down North America's giant redwoods and whales were being hunted in their thousands. But, slowly, people began to realize that these resources could disappear for good. In 1946, whaling was regulated for the first time, and later, in the 1970s, environmental groups such as Greenpeace and Friends of the Earth were born. Their early campaigns marked the start of the modern environmental age.

Compost bin for organic kitchen waste

Solar collectors contain a network of water-filled pipes. Sunlight heats the water, which is then stored in a large tank.

Surplus electricity generated by the house is supplied to the national grid through an underground cable.

The sun-facing side of the house has large windows, to capture as much sunshine as possible during winter.

Pollution-free, hydrogen-powered car (see page 51)

▼ For most of the year, this house generates all the energy that it needs, using technology that is available today. It is powered by sunlight — the ultimate renewable resource. Where possible, the house is built from local materials, helping to reduce the amount of pollution caused by construction and transport.

Photovoltaic cells on the roof turn sunlight directly into electricity, powering all the domestic appliances.

A small wind turbine provides back-up power in cloudy weather.

Insulated wooden walls help to keep the house warm in winter and cool in summer. The insulation is made from recycled materials, helping to reduce construction costs and waste.

Renewables at home

In a sustainable world, changes would begin at home. The house shown on these two pages is designed with sustainable living in mind. It is well insulated, to keep it warm in winter, and most of the energy it needs is provided by solar collectors and photovoltaic cells (see pages 50–51). In sunny conditions, a house like this would make surplus electricity, which would be fed to the national grid. Cutting down on waste is also an important part of 'green' living. In this house, food waste goes to make garden compost, while paper, metals and plastics are sorted so they can be recycled. For more details about recycling, see pages 52–53.

A shared responsibility

If all new homes were like this, it would do a lot to conserve the world's resources. On a personal level, you can help by the choices you make, because 'green' consumers encourage businesses to change. But no matter how careful you are, you will not be able to stop all of the environmental problems that affect the world today. Some are simply far too big. That is why many green groups want governments to set tougher rules. They believe that businesses should share in the global clean-up, by taking responsibility for environmental problems that they cause.

Tiny microprocessors positioned throughout the house are linked to a central computer. They automatically adjust lighting and heating levels by sensing conditions both indoors and outside.

A rain-collecting system provides enough water for bathing, dishwashing, flushing and laundry. Waste water from the kitchen and shower is used to irrigate the garden, instead of being disposed of with sewage.

Under-floor heating, using piped water from the main tank, distributes warmth evenly throughout the house.

▶ Direct action has helped to put environmental issues in the headlines. Here, Greenpeace volunteers are protesting about air pollution from the top of an incinerator chimney.

Science to the rescue?

During the last 50 years, technology has revolutionized the way we live. Could it also help to overcome some of the environmental problems that we face? Many scientists think so. But technology has its limits: sometimes the best way to fix a problem is not to make things more complicated, but simpler and more safe.

Closing the ozone hole

When scientists discovered the ozone hole, in the 1980s, they realized that rapid action was needed to repair it. The hole was caused mainly by CFCs (see page 37), so it was vital that these chemicals were phased out. It seemed an almost impossible task, but effective substitutes to CFCs were found, and an international agreement – the Montreal Protocol – was drawn up to set a timetable for the change. Thanks to this agreement, and to new technology, a major environmental crisis was successfully averted.

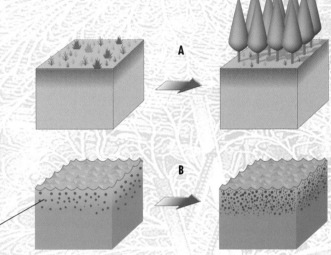

Algae

▲ If plant growth is given a boost, extra carbon dioxide is removed from the air, helping to reverse the greenhouse effect. Planting trees is a tried-and-tested way of doing this (diagram A). Encouraging algae by fertilizing the oceans could also help (diagram B), but it might have unwanted side effects on marine life.

▲ This false-colour satellite image shows the density of microscopic algae – which absorb carbon dioxide – in the world's oceans. Red areas have the most algae, while light blue has the least.

Fighting global warming

Global warming presents an even bigger challenge than the ozone hole, because it goes to the very heart of modern life. Somehow we have to reduce the atmosphere's carbon dioxide level, and it is possible that new technology could help. One high-tech solution, first suggested in the 1990s, involves 'fertilizing' the oceans with iron to boost the growth of algae, which absorb carbon dioxide from the air. Another involves storing carbon dioxide by pumping it into the ground. These schemes look good on paper, and energy companies like them, because they mean we could continue to burn fossil fuels. But many experts doubt that they would really work on a global scale. A much simpler way of locking up carbon is to plant new forests. Better still, we could tackle the source of the problem by using renewable energy, which produces no carbon dioxide at all.

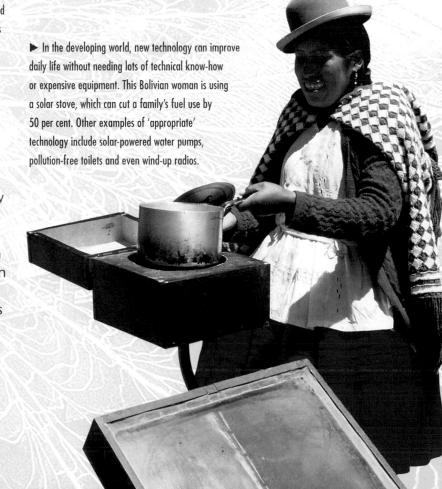

▲ Electricity flashes around the Z Machine, an experimental device used in nuclear fusion research. The machine can heat gases to a temperature of nearly ten million degrees Celsius – almost hot enough to trigger nuclear fusion, which would release massive amounts of power.

◄ A research scientist checks a field of genetically modified wheat. GM technology allows scientists to move useful genes between different species – something that traditional breeding techniques cannot do.

The ultimate energy source

In the world of high-tech science, the quest to harness nuclear fusion is one of the most ambitious projects of all. Nuclear fusion makes the sun shine, so it is a process that keeps all of us alive. Unlike nuclear fission, which involves splitting atoms, fusion forces them together. As the atoms fuse, they give off a colossal amount of energy, but they produce no carbon dioxide and very little dangerous waste. Some physicists believe that fusion could be the ultimate answer to the world's energy needs. Building a fusion reactor is an immensely difficult task, however. Despite years of research, fusion power has still not got off the ground.

► In the developing world, new technology can improve daily life without needing lots of technical know-how or expensive equipment. This Bolivian woman is using a solar stove, which can cut a family's fuel use by 50 per cent. Other examples of 'appropriate' technology include solar-powered water pumps, pollution-free toilets and even wind-up radios.

Farming and food

So far, the world's countries have been unable to agree a global warming action plan. They also disagree about new ways of growing food. One argument is about the use of chemicals: organic farmers try to avoid them altogether, because they can damage the environment and end up in human food. Another dispute concerns genetic modification (GM) – a new technology that can create special varieties of animals and plants. As the human population continues to grow, some scientists think that GM technology could be the answer to the world's food problems. Others are firmly opposed to it, because modified varieties could contaminate and damage wild species. At present, the arguments have reached a bad-tempered stalemate. GM crops are widely grown in North America, but they are tightly controlled or even banned in some countries.

Renewable energy

Today, nearly all of the energy we use comes
from fossil fuels or nuclear power. But in future,
we will depend far more on renewable sources,
such as sunlight, wind and waves. Renewable
energy is not free, and sometimes it is not quite
as 'green' as it seems. But unlike other sources
of energy, it keeps being replaced, so it can
be harvested forever without running out.

▶ When it is finished, the
Three Gorges dam on China's
Yangtze river will be one of
the biggest in the world. As
well as generating electricity,
it will stop the Yangtze's
notorious floods, which have
claimed countless lives.

Solar power

Sunlight is by far the biggest source of renewable energy.
It is safe and non-polluting, and in theory it could meet
all our energy needs. Unfortunately, sunlight is not easy to
harvest on a large scale, which is why solar power stations
are rare. On a local scale, using solar energy is much more
practical. It can be gathered by solar collectors, which heat
water, and by photovoltaic cells, which convert light into
electricity. Photovoltaic cells are particularly useful, because
they can be installed almost anywhere, from roofs to the
tops of utility poles. In decades to come, solar power looks
likely to expand in a major way, as the price of photovoltaic
cells comes down and their efficiency goes up.

Hydropower

Compared to other renewable energy sources, hydroelectric
power already makes a big impact. Gigantic dams straddle
the world's largest rivers, generating electricity for millions
of factories and homes. A dam can produce pollution-free
power for decades, and it can also help to supply drinking
water and prevent floods and droughts. However, big dams
cost an immense amount to build, and their reservoirs often
flood natural habitats, farmland and homes. Hydropower
will remain important in the future, but tomorrow's dams
are likely to be smaller than those being built today.

Wind and waves

Centuries ago, windmills were common in some countries.
Today, their place has been taken by wind turbines, which
generate electricity with slender rotating blades. Wind power
is not cheap, but it has one key advantage: the wind is often
strongest in winter, when electric power is needed most.
But the wind is unreliable, and sometimes does not blow
at all. Many engineers think that wave power has a brighter
future, because waves contain much more energy. However,
wave turbines are still in their experimental phase.

▲ The Solar One power station, near Barstow in California, USA, collects sunlight
with 1,800 steerable, computer-controlled mirrors. The sunlight is used to make
steam, and this powers a turbine that generates enough electricity for 5,000 homes.

▶ These two students in Benin are maintaining a biogas digester – a simple device that produces methane gas from plant and animal waste. The gas is stored in tanks, and is used for cooking and lighting. Biogas systems are cheap to install and easy to run, making them ideal for people living in rural areas.

◀ Green campaigners have divided views about wind turbines. Some are enthusiastic about them, but others feel they spoil landscapes and harm wildlife without generating much energy in return.

The hydrogen world

Renewable energy has one big drawback: unlike oil, it cannot be carried about. If we are really going to cut back on fossil fuels, a substitute for oil has to be found. That substitute will almost certainly be liquid hydrogen – a pressurized gas that is already being used to power some buses and cars. Hydrogen can be made from water, and it produces no pollution at all when it burns. To make it, electrical energy is needed, and that is where renewable sources play a part. In tomorrow's 'hydrogen world', sunshine could be used to make this ideal fuel. As oil is slowly phased out, the days of smoking exhausts and polluted air would become a distant memory.

▶ At this experimental filling station in Germany, a car fills up with liquid hydrogen instead of petrol. On a full tank, it can travel 300km. The hydrogen gas is produced by a bank of photovoltaic cells, and it is pressurized to turn it into a liquid.

Reuse and recycling

What is the difference between a bottle made of brand-new glass, and one made from glass that has been recycled? The answer is very little, apart from the impact that they have on the environment. Recycling saves raw materials, and it cuts down on waste and pollution. Reusing objects helps the environment even more. Today, recycling is still patchy, and too much is thrown away, but in tomorrow's world it will play an increasing part in reducing household waste.

A recycling line-up

Glass and metals are perfect for recycling, because they can be melted down and reused almost indefinitely. Paper is not quite so good, because its fibres gradually weaken each time it is used. As a result, it can be recycled only about six or seven times. But even that is a huge saving for the environment, so recycling paper makes good sense. Plastics are much more problematic, because there are so many different kinds. Very few can be melted down and made into the same thing again and again. Instead, many plastics are recycled just once, by being made into objects such as carrier bags or drainage pipes. After that, they are usually thrown away. For a world drowning in waste, it is a problem that must be solved.

▶ Colour-coded recycling bins are already a common sight, and they are set to become more widespread. In the future, many plastics will go into the same bin as kitchen waste, because they will be biodegradable.

◀ These wine bottles contain over 50 per cent recycled glass. New glass takes a lot of energy to make, so adding recycled glass reduces the pollution caused by burning fossil fuels.

Compost from waste

Unlike plastics, a lot of household waste is already biodegradable, because nature made it that way. Food and garden waste can all be turned into compost, a natural fertilizer that is spread on fields. At present, only a small amount of household waste ends up being composted, but with landfill sites overflowing, that is likely to change. To make this kind of recycling feasible, waste has to be pre-sorted. Many of us already do this, but local authorities will need to encourage people who do not seem to have the time. One possibility might be to charge people according to how much unrecyclable rubbish they throw away. When that happens, being wasteful will not just be shortsighted – it will be expensive too.

Plastics that rot away

One way of reducing plastic waste is to cut down on packaging that nobody needs, and some countries have introduced charges for throwaway plastic bags. Better still, scientists are trying to devise new kinds of biodegradable plastics, which rot down harmlessly when they are thrown away. Normal plastics are made from oil, but biodegradable plastics are usually made from plant-based products, such as corn starch or cellulose. The challenge is to turn these substances into plastics that are as strong as the ones we use today. Scientists have not got there yet, but the race is on. Success will be well worth the effort, because the market for these plastics could be worth 25 billion US dollars a year.

▲ Disposable cutlery (background image) can be made from recycled plastic, but after being used it is normally thrown away. This is an example of 'open-loop' recycling. In 'closed-loop' recycling, a raw material – such as glass – can be recycled an unlimited number of times.

▼ This bale contains shredded waste paper, ready to be recycled. At one time, old newspapers were useless waste, but thanks to recycling they have become a useful commodity.

Wildlife protection

Across the globe, thousands of different organizations are working hard to protect animals and plants that are under threat. There have been some great successes, with endangered species pulled back from the very edge of extinction. Some of these success stories could soon be off the danger list altogether. But protecting wildlife involves some difficult questions. What is the best way of helping threatened species? And how can we leave space for wildlife when so many people are short of space themselves?

▲ Costa Rica is one of the world leaders in conservation. Over a quarter of this Central American country is protected by wildlife reserves, such as the Rincón de la Vieja national park (above).

Species or habitats?

Many wildlife campaigns focus on particular species, such as giant pandas, orang utans or whales. Without this work, some of these animals might now be extinct in the wild. But with so many species in danger, we cannot afford a separate scheme for each one. Instead, conservationists now give top priority to saving complete habitats, so that all their species can look after themselves. Some reserves are truly vast. One of the largest, Canada's Wood Buffalo national park, covers 45,000km² – an area as big as Switzerland.

Stopping the wildlife trade

Saving wildlife means tough action against people who exploit endangered species. Over 160 countries have signed the Convention on International Trade in Endangered Species (CITES), which bans cross-border trade in over 2,500 animal species, and nearly ten times as many plants. In ports and airports worldwide, customs officers keep watch for species on the CITES lists, and also for their body parts, such as fur, ivory, shells and bones. Soon, DNA testing could help them to identify listed species.

Controlling introduced species

Conservation sometimes involves undoing past mistakes. In some countries, a huge effort is made to control introduced species that harm native wildlife. In South Africa, the worst invaders are trees and shrubs, which have to be cut down and burned. In Australia, the main offenders are predators, such as foxes. They are trapped, or killed with a poison that is harmless to native animals. This is controversial, but scientists are convinced it will help Australia's rarest animals to survive.

◀ In 1989, a pile of confiscated tusks was publicly burned in Kenya to publicize the fight against the illegal elephant ivory trade. Ivory fetches a high price on the black market: this pile had a street value of about 750,000 US dollars.

Emergency action

When a species is in really dire straits, drastic measures may be needed to save it. Captive breeding has proved successful with some critically endangered mammals and birds, such as the California condor. In 1987, there were just 27 left in zoos, with none in the wild. But by 2004, the population had risen to 215, and about 80 birds had been released from captivity. Sometimes, endangered animals are moved to safer homes. The tuatara – a rare lizard from New Zealand – was airlifted from the mainland to several offshore islands, where it does not have to face predatory mammals. With endangered plants, seeds can be stored in special seed banks, where they stay alive for years. This biological 'insurance' makes sure that the species lives on.

▲ Using a hand puppet, a keeper feeds a California condor chick at San Diego zoo, USA. The young birds are kept away from people so that they will be able to fend for themselves in the wild.

Making wildlife pay

To survive in the long term, wildlife needs to be wild. But in our overcrowded world, people need space too. Somehow we have to find a way of living with wildlife, instead of pushing it aside. One possible solution is to make wildlife pay. The national parks of Costa Rica have become an important economic asset, because they attract lots of foreign visitors. In southern Africa, tourists flock to see elephants and rhinos, while all over the world, from North America to Australia, people pay for the unbeatable excitement of watching whales. Tourism cannot protect all the world's wildlife, and it can cause environmental problems of its own. But if it is carefully managed, tourism could help to preserve rare species in tomorrow's world.

◀ Peering down at the floating sea ice, a party of tourists heads towards the coast of Antarctica. Tourism is booming in this far-flung continent, but visitors have to follow strict guidelines to prevent harm to its wildlife. Animals here are often tame, but touching or feeding them is forbidden.

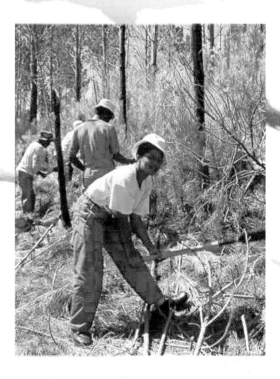

▲ In South Africa, a scrub-clearance team hacks away at invading plants that are smothering native vegetation. The entrance fees charged by national parks help to fund this important work.

The future

By the year 2100, the world's population may have stopped growing, but there could be twice as many people as there are now. With so many humans needing food and somewhere to live, the pressure on our planet will be intense. So what will planet earth be like? Will it be more polluted, with species disappearing at an ever-faster rate? Or will it be on the road to recovery after all the mistakes of the past? Although 2100 is a long way off, the future depends on decisions that are being made today.

Global co-operation

In 2004, over 120 countries signed an ambitious agreement that aims to save endangered species and their habitats. Within six years, each country is expected to have at least ten per cent of its land under protection, and by 2012, ocean life will be included as well. If things go to plan, the outlook will be much better for the world's wildlife. On other fronts, talks are under way to control all kinds of environmental problems, from packaging waste to pollution at sea. This truly international effort is a promising sign for the planet's future.

Business as usual

Unfortunately, agreeing to do something is not the same as doing it. Environmental agreements can be hard to enforce, and they cost money. Whenever there is a choice between big business and the environment, business often seems to win. Tropical rainforests highlight this dilemma: despite being some of the world's richest wildlife habitats, they are disappearing fast as loggers, farmers and miners move in. In the fight to preserve them, local conservationists literally risk their lives.

▶ Without action to save the environment, earth's future looks grim. The next 100 years could bring a collapse in the world's biological diversity, as habitats become fragmented and global warming takes its toll. In this kind of world, the lucky minority would live in comfort, but a host of environmental problems — from water pollution to soil erosion — would make life extremely difficult for most people. Today, this global split has already begun.

Piling on the pressure

During the coming century, the natural world will be under pressure in other ways. In rapidly developing countries, such as China and India, millions of newly prosperous people will become western-style consumers. They will expect the same services and products that westerners enjoy, such as air travel, fast cars and fast food. By 2100, global food production will have to double – an awesome challenge that could have serious side effects for other living things. As well as being efficient, agriculture will have to be much more reliable: if not, billions of the world's poorest people could face famines far worse than the ones that occur today.

Differing opinions

Some experts think that rising prosperity is the key to solving the planet's problems. If they are right, in 2100 the earth will be busier, more built up, but less polluted than today. In this future world, human ingenuity would help to safeguard wildlife, and problems such as global warming would be under control. But many environmentalists are not convinced by this picture. Without strong action, they believe that most of the world's tropical rainforests could vanish in the next 50 years, followed by other threatened habitats, such as wetlands and coral reefs. By 2100, some people might well be more prosperous, but the world as a whole could be a much poorer place.

An ecological future

The future is notoriously difficult to predict, and even the experts can be wrong. In the 1960s, for example, some scientists predicted a population catastrophe by the year 2000, with people struggling to survive on an overloaded earth. Others thought that people would be living permanently on the Moon by 2000. Both predictions turned out to be wrong, and so will many of the predictions that are made today. As we look forwards into the future, however, there are two pieces of genuinely good news. The first is that nature is incredibly resilient, and can bounce back if it is given a chance. The second is that millions of people now care passionately about the environment. In a world affected by many problems, that is the most promising sign of all.

◀ If humans manage to master the art of sustainable living, tomorrow's world could be less polluted than today's – despite a huge increase in the global population. In this kind of world, energy would come almost entirely from renewable resources, and all everyday products, from cars to computers, would be designed to be recycled once their useful life was over. The world's surviving wilderness areas would be fully protected from exploitation, just like Antarctica is today.

SUMMARY OF CHAPTER 3: SUSTAINABLE WORLD

Sustainable living

For most of human history, people have been bad at conserving the world's resources, and even worse at preventing pollution and waste. This has created a range of environmental problems, which were explored in chapter 2. This chapter looked at possible solutions to these problems, involving changes in the way people live. The goal of these changes is sustainability. In other words, they focus on resources that can be renewed or recycled, instead of ones that are used once and then thrown away.

As solar power technology improves, sunlight will meet more of our energy needs in the future.

Scientific solutions

In the search for sustainability, science has an important role to play. Improvements in technology mean that it is becoming easier and cheaper to harness energy from renewable sources, such as sunlight, wind or waves. In the future, hydrogen technology could make driving almost pollution-free, and biodegradable plastics and improved recycling facilities could reduce the problem of waste. But technology will not provide all the answers. Without careful testing, some scientific advances – such as the genetic modification of crops and livestock – could make environmental problems worse.

Making the switch

In the 21st century, the human population could almost double before it finally levels out. At the same time, global warming will become more noticeable, creating problems for the living world. These changes are already under way, so we cannot escape their effects. But concern about the environment is beginning to spur people and governments into action. If humans make the switch to a sustainable way of life – in which species and habitats are protected and resources are conserved – our planet could be on the road to recovery.

Go further...

Visit the UN Environment Programme's youth site – a great place to find out what young people are doing to safeguard the planet: www.unep.org/Documents/Default.asp?DocumentID=295

For the latest news about Friends of the Earth's environmental campaigns, visit its UK website: www.foe.co.uk

The Greenpeace International website is full of information about environmental issues and direct action taken by Greenpeace volunteers: www.greenpeace.org/international_en

Environmental campaigner
Raises awareness about environmental problems, sometimes by direct action.

Environmental consultant
Advises companies about environmental problems and ways to avoid them.

Futurologist
Predicts the future by analyzing current trends.

Geneticist
Studies genes, DNA and inheritance.

Wildlife ranger
Conserves wildlife by working in natural parks and reserves.

See wildlife rescue in action by visiting Whipsnade Wild Animal Park. Run by the Zoological Society of London, it is famous for its work with endangered species. Whipsnade Wild Animal Park Dunstable, Bedfordshire LU6 2LF, UK Telephone: +44 (0) 1582 872171 www.whipsnade.co.uk

Visit the Centre for Alternative Technology – Europe's leading eco-centre – to see demonstrations of all kinds of environment-friendly inventions, from home wind turbines to reedbed waste treatment plants. Centre for Alternative Technology Machynlleth, Powys SY20 9AZ, UK Telephone: +44 (0) 1654 705950 www.cat.org.uk

Glossary

acid rain
Rain that has been made acidic by pollutants in the air.

adaptation
In living things, any feature that has been produced by evolution. Adaptations help living things to survive and reproduce.

alga (plural: algae)
Simple, plant-like organisms that grow by collecting the energy in sunlight. Most algae live in water.

'appropriate' technology
Technology that draws on local resources and skills, instead of those that are brought in from other parts of the world.

aquifer
A natural reservoir of underground water. The water is usually held in small pores and cracks in rocks.

atmosphere
The blanket of gases that surrounds the earth. The atmosphere is composed mainly of nitrogen and oxygen, with small amounts of other gases, such as water vapour and carbon dioxide.

atom
The smallest particle of an element, such as carbon, from which all matter is made.

bacterium (plural: bacteria)
A microbe with a single cell. Bacteria are the smallest, simplest and most ancient living things on earth.

biodegradable
A word that describes anything which can be broken down and digested by living things.

biodiversity
The number of different species in a given area, or on the planet as a whole.

biome
A characteristic community of plants and animals, such as grassland, desert or tropical rainforest.

biosphere
All the parts of the world where living things are found.

broadleaved tree
A tree that usually has broad, flat leaves, such as an oak, beech or eucalyptus. Unlike conifers, broadleaved trees are flowering plants.

bromeliad
A type of plant with stiff, spiky leaves that often grows on tree trunks and branches.

canopy
The upper layer of a forest, formed by the interlocking branches of neighbouring trees.

carbon
A chemical element found in all living things. Carbon forms thousands of different compounds in nature. Thousands more – including plastics, solvents and medicines – have been made artificially by chemists.

carbon dioxide
A colourless, carbon-containing gas. It is taken in by plants when they carry out photosynthesis, and given out by animals when they release energy from food.

cellulose
A carbon-containing substance that plants make and use as a building material.

CFC
Short for chlorofluorocarbon, CFCs are man-made compounds that can destroy the ozone layer.

compost
A crumbly mixture containing the remains of plants, as well as the microbes that break them down. Compost is good for improving the fertility of soil.

compound
A chemical that contains atoms of several elements, combined in a particular way.

conserve
To minimize the use of any natural resource, such as tropical trees or a fossil fuel, so that it does not run out.

Logging in North America

continental drift
The gradual movement of continents across the earth's surface.

decompose
To rot down. In nature, decomposition is carried out by bacteria and other microbes, which break down and recycle dead remains.

deforestation
The permanent removal of forest, often to make way for farmland.

demographic transition
A slowdown in population growth that occurs when a country becomes developed.

developed country
A country with high average incomes and with well-developed services, such as hospitals and schools. Most developed countries are industrialized.

developing country
A country where average incomes are low and where many people do not have access to basic services, such as clean water and education.

endemic species
A species that is found in only one place.

environment
The setting around any living thing. The word 'environment' can also be used in a much wider sense, to mean the setting for the whole of the living world.

Sprawling suburbs, Mexico City

evolution
A very slow process of change that enables living things to adapt to the world around them. During evolution, new species develop and existing ones eventually become extinct.

extinction
The permanent disappearance of a species.

fossil
The preserved remains of living things. Some fossils are formed by remains, while others are signs that living things leave behind, such as burrows or footprints.

fossil fuels
Fuels formed in sedimentary rocks by the fossilized remains of prehistoric plants that lived millions of years ago. Fossil fuels include oil, coal and natural gas.

gene
A chemical instruction passed on from parents to their offspring when living things breed. Genes help to build living things, and they control the way they work.

genetic modification (GM)
A way of giving a living thing new features by inserting genes from another species.

global warming
A worldwide rise in temperatures caused by the build-up of the greenhouse effect.

'green'
A label used for people or political parties that are committed to helping the natural environment.

greenhouse effect
A feature of the atmosphere that blocks heat escaping into space. The greenhouse effect keeps the earth much warmer than it would otherwise be.

groundwater
Water that flows through spaces deep underground. See also **aquifer**.

habitat
The surroundings that a particular species needs to survive. Most species live in just one habitat, but some can survive in several.

herbicide
Any chemical that kills plants.

hydroelectric power
Electric power that is generated by moving water. The electricity is produced by turbines at the base of a dam.

hydrological cycle
The natural cycle that replenishes all the freshwater on earth. It begins when heat from the sun evaporates seawater, and turns it into rain or snow.

industrialized country
A country where most people work in factories and offices, and few work on the land.

intensive farming
Farming that produces high yields, but which depends on a lot of herbicides, fertilizer and fuel.

introduced species
A species that has been spread by people to a region where it does not naturally occur.

landfill
A site where waste is disposed of by piling it up and then covering it with earth.

methane
A colourless gas that is produced when things rot down in swampy ground.

microbe
Any living thing that is too small to be seen with the naked eye, such as a bacterium.

mineral
A naturally occurring chemical in the earth's crust. Mixtures of minerals make up rocks.

nitrogen
The most abundant gas in the atmosphere. Nitrogen is an important ingredient in proteins, so it is needed by all living things.

Young giant panda, China

photovoltaic cell
A device that converts the energy in light directly into electricity.

recycling
Reprocessing any product so that its raw materials can be used again.

Red Data Lists
Lists of threatened species, prepared and updated by the International Union for the Conservation of Nature and Natural Resources (IUCN).

reserves
Stocks of fuels or minerals that are known to exist, but which have not yet been extracted and used.

species
A single type of living thing. The members of a species can all breed with each other, but they do not normally breed with anything else.

sulphur dioxide
An acid gas that is produced when sulphur-containing fuels, such as coal, are burned.

nitrous oxide
A compound of nitrogen produced when fuels are burned. Along with other nitrogen oxides, it is a major cause of air pollution in places where there is heavy traffic.

nuclear fission
A way of producing energy by splitting atoms of heavy elements, such as uranium. Nuclear fission produces waste that remains dangerously radioactive for many years.

nuclear fusion
A method of producing energy by forcing atoms to fuse, or combine.

organic farming
A way of farming that tries to use land in a sustainable way. Organic farmers do not use artificial fertilizers or herbicides.

ozone
A poisonous, colourless gas that contains the same kind of atoms as oxygen. High in the atmosphere, the ozone layer absorbs harmful rays in sunlight.

ozone hole
A gap in the ozone layer caused by man-made chemicals, such as CFCs, that have escaped into the air.

pesticide
Any chemical designed to kill animals, such as insects, that attack crops or livestock.

photochemical smog
A brown haze produced when strong sunlight falls on polluted air. The energy in the sunlight makes pollutants react with each other.

photosynthesis
A process that plants, algae and some bacteria use to grow. During photosynthesis, they collect energy from sunlight, and use it to make complex chemicals from carbon dioxide and water.

sustainable
A word used to describe an activity that continues indefinitely without running out of the things that it needs to work.

vertebrate
An animal that has a backbone. Vertebrates include fish, amphibians, reptiles, birds and mammals.

Fossilized skull of a
Tyrannosaurus rex

Index

Acknowledgements

The publisher would like to thank the following for permission to reproduce their material. Every care has been taken to trace copyright holders. However, if there have been unintentional omissions or failure to trace copyright holders, we apologize and will, if informed, endeavour to make corrections in any future edition.

Key: *b* = bottom, *c* = centre, *l* = left, *r* = right, *t* = top

Cover *l* Lonely Planet Images; cover *c* Nature History Picture Agency; cover *r* Corbis; 1 Still Pictures (Still); 2–3 Edifice; 4–5 Still; 7 Corbis; 8–9 Getty Stone; 8*tr* Getty Imagebank; 9*tr* Science Photo Library (SPL); 10–11 Lonely Planet; 10*bl* Still; 11*cl* SPL; 11*br* Nature Picture Library (Naturepl); 12 SPL; 13 Sue Cunningham; 14 Lonely Planet; 15*br* Lonely Planet; 16*tl* Corbis; 16*bl* Still; 16*bc* Still; 17 Getty Stone; 18 Lonely Planet; 19 Still; 20–21 Corbis; 20 Corbis; 21*t* Corbis; 22–23 Corbis; 22*bl* Still; 23*tr* Corbis; 24*br* Corbis; 24–25 Corbis; 25*tc* Lonely Planet; 25*tr* Lonely Planet; 26–27 Corbis; 26*cl* Corbis; 26–27*t* Corbis; 27*tr* Corbis; 28–29 Getty Taxi; 28–29*t* Corbis; 30–31 Corbis; 30*tl* Corbis; 31*tl* Corbis; 31*br* Still; 32*bl* Still; 32–33*t* Still; 33*tr* Lonely Planet; 33*b* Still; 34–35 Getty Imagebank; 34 Corbis; 35*tr* Still; 36–37 Alamy; 36*bl* SPL; 38*tl* Corbis; 38*bl* SPL; 39*tl* Alamy; 39*tr* SPL; 39*br* Corbis; 40–41 Getty Imagebank; 41*cl* Lonely Planet; 41*br* Zefa; 42–43*t* Lonely Planet; 42*cl* Ardea; 42*b* Getty Taxi; 43*br* Alamy; 44 Corbis; 45 Ecoscene; 46 Art Archive; 47*br* Greenpeace; 48–49*t* Sandia National Laboratories; 48*bl* SPL; 49*cl* Getty Stone; 49*br* Lonely Planet; 50–51 Corbis; 50*bl* SPL; 50–51*t* Corbis; 51*tr* Still; 51*br* SPL; 52–53 Alamy; 53*tl* Alamy; 53*tr* Alamy; 53*b* Zefa; 54*tl* Corbis; 54*bl* Oxford Scientific Films; 54–55*b* Getty Imagebank; 55*tr* Corbis; 58 SPL; 59 Corbis; 60*bl* Corbis; 61*t* National Geographic Society; 61*b* SPL; 64 Still

The publisher would like to thank the following illustrators:
Steve Weston (Linden Artists); Encompass Graphics; Peter Clayman